When a Child Dies, Love Remains

Hertifacts

MAGGIE HORGAN

HEARTIFACTS

When a Child Dies,
Love Remains

Written by: Maggie Horgan
Inspired by: Neil Christopher

ISBN: 1495365328
ISBN 13: 9781495365324
Library of Congress Control Number: 2014901825
CreateSpace Independent Publishing Platform,
North Charleston, South Carolina

Dedicated to my children

**Lauren, 8, Neil, 15, Gregory, 4, and
Davin, 13, (November 1996)**

ACKNOWLEDGEMENTS

I approach the task of acknowledging everyone who was involved in the evolution of *Heartifacts* with trepidation; I hope no one is overlooked in the process, and I beg forgiveness in advance should that actually occur. There is no end to the gratitude I feel as I write this page.

I must first thank Reverend Richard L. Freeman Sr. and the rest of the Memorial Service Planning Committee of the Children's Hospital of Pittsburgh. In April of 2005, they were the first to encourage me to share my grief journey. Frankly, I never knew I had a story to tell until I participated in the loving service they offered to the bereaved families I met there. Next, I thank my family, friends and many of the grieving families who heard my message and encouraged me to carry on. Were it not for all of those who bolstered my efforts along the way, this work might never have made it to you.

I received compassionate and constructive encouragement from a myriad of manuscript readers. This group includes my father, James Francis Horgan (now deceased), several of my eleven siblings, a few brave nieces and nephews, all of my children, and a bouquet of very special friends: Kalin Gabrielle Alberts, Sheryl Blumenthal, John A. Caputo, Esq., Judy Ann Carlin, Judith (Kirsch) Ciesielski, Barbara (Fogarty) and Bruce Fisher, Sunny Disney Fitchett, Ruth G. Foltz,

Mary Beth (Kelly) Gasior, Petrea (Rieck) Graham, Eileen (Kennedy) and Alan Levine, Cyndi (Schoeppner) McGinnis, Lisa (DeRose) and Robert Pompeani, Judith Wolf-Skopek, Stanley G. Scalise, Bradley J. Stewart, Jacqueline (Taylor) Strasbaugh, Dana (Depasqua) Williott, and Coach Michael E. Wilson.

In addition to these extraordinary people, Jennifer Bridy Carroll provided the book outline that got my thoughts off the starting block and onto paper, Penda L. James, M.Ed., did invaluable preliminary editing, Lisa Michelle LeRose graphically edited all of my archival photographs, and Edward A. Witt, Esq., photographed my collection of heartifacts for the book's cover.

Several testimonials have been provided at the end of *Heartifacts* for which I am thoroughly grateful, as well. For these I thank the following generous and thoughtful individuals: Sr. Lisa Balcerek, CSJ, Ms. Diane S. Hupp, MSN, RN, NEA-BC, Mrs. Cyndi McGinnis, Mr. Michael Shulock, MS, CCLS, Mrs. Shari L. Wilson, and Ms. Carol May, RN, MSN, MBA, CHPN.

Finally, I owe a special thank you to James F. Waldron Jr. for inspiring me to take this endeavor across the finish line once and for all. He compassionately nudged me in the right direction by connecting me with Hollis T. Hurd, Esq., an experienced CreateSpace author. Without hesitation, Mr. Hurd contacted me and demystified self-publishing. (Truthfully, his direction gave me the courage to engage the process.) The professionals at CreateSpace, in turn, handled my work and me with great care.

Thanks to the steadfast support of God's loving spirit and all the people who kept me moving in a positive direction, I now present *Heartifacts*. I pray that it will inspire anyone who survives a child to open their hearts for the healing to come and the peace that is possible.

CONTENTS

FOREWORD

In the midst of a wonderful fourteen-year journey as a pediatric chaplain, I have witnessed the depths of despair and heights of recovery that the grief experience can afford. The most unwanted guest called Death does not spare anyone. However, the death of a child violates the very fiber of hope that is resident in the heart of every parent. "I'm supposed to go first" is a refrain I have heard so often in the midst of overwhelming sobs. Parents' hearts are inflicted with a wound from which many believe they will never recover.

I had the honor of encountering Maggie in the midst of such a journey. The brilliant star that is her son, Neil, had been reduced to a valiant ember by the devastating onslaught of cancer. Maggie too asked the ubiquitous question, "Why?" When Neil's earthly battle came to a truncated end, Maggie had to find the motivation to move forward with life—a life that had just treated her, her son, and her family in the most awful manner. As a person of faith, I seek to transfer the hope resident in faith by concluding my journey with families with the statement, "You are going to make it through!" It is an expression of hope without a clue as to the specifics that the recovery will take. I just believe in the capacity of a loving, caring God to help us through the journey of grief and bereavement even when all seems hopeless.

Heartifacts is the record of just such a journey, and the beauty of the book's message is its universality. Indeed, if we but listen, it speaks to the journey of grief and bereavement any of us will traverse. Maggie pours out of her heart how her faith, the spirit of Neil, the compassion of God, and the warm hardness of heart stones have led her to a recovered place. *Heartifacts* displays the confluence of faith, hope, and love. It challenges the often used phrase, "I need closure." Maggie cannot close the door on a love so deep and complete. The *Heartifacts* journey shares how God chose to promote healing in the spirit of His child, Maggie Horgan.

Maggie has offered glimpses of the *Heartifacts* journey to hundreds of bereaved parents, grandparents, aunts, uncles, and siblings as she has spoken on a number of occasions at our twice-annual memorial services here at our hospital. I have witnessed and many people have attested to the healing balm nestled in the *Heartifacts* narrative. I hope you will embrace the journey toward healing...a journey embodied in *Heartifacts*.

Reverend Richard L. Freeman Sr.
Manager, Pastoral Care
Children's Hospital of Pittsburgh of UPMC
Senior Pastor, Resurrection Baptist Church

heartifact

(här'-ti-fakt) n. 1. An inspired, uncontrived, and perfectly timed heart-shaped reminder of love's eternal nature—especially love that connects living human beings to their deceased loved ones (*particularly children*). 2. A heart-shaped token of loyalty, compassion, healing, and love created through the earth's natural processes (i.e., erosion, tides, weather, etc.). Examples of nature's heartifacts include: stones, rocks, seashells, coral, plants, and clouds bearing the shape of a heart. 3. Spiritual, mystical, supernatural, powerful, and meaningful heart-shaped representations of grace from God. Note: Heartifacts have divine and miraculous qualities.

Heartifacts

(här'-ti-fakts) n. 1. The book written to preserve one mother's compelling story of how uncontrived, nature-made hearts poignantly manifested in her life following the death of her son. 2. The legend of the unexpected heart stones that spirited a grieving mother along on her journey of healing. 3. A story of faith and endurance.

GATHERING HOPE

Writing *Heartifacts* has taken years and included the fine-tuning of many manuscripts. That is to say, I grew up with many dreams, but writing a book concerning grief was never one of them. When Neil died, my dreams changed. *Everything changed*. He was my firstborn.

I am fairly certain there are no adequate words of consolation for grieving parents, yet I have written the following chapters in an effort to do just that. The reason is simple: I have more than words to offer. By 2001, unbearable loss wedged itself into my family and my life, but during the balance of that same year, so did an infusion of remarkable tokens of hope. I call them heartifacts.

The moment I held my first heartifact, I knew death had not consumed Neil's spirit and grief was not to consume mine. The unique and unexpected heart-shaped stone also fortified me as I coped with my demanding new companion, grief…and not a moment too soon. Along with my surviving children, I had been through too much during the previous three years and was overwhelmed in the aftermath. Thankfully, heartifacts still surface when we least expect them, and we never tire of them. They remind us Neil is close.

Besides grief being a baseline challenge, my "rational" mind was not much help to me as I struggled to complete this book. I reasoned that others less intimate with grief might categorize me as someone who had gone off the deep end.

"Let them," I finally decided.

This is a book about finding hope when life gets crazy, and from my perspective, the message could not be more timely. We live in a puzzling world.

Besides my superego getting in the way of my writing, attacks of gut-wrenching grief interrupted my efforts with predictable randomness at the outset. Over time, I befriended predictable randomness and decided to regard grief as I would an opportunistic bully. I did not like grief, and I wanted it gone, but it wasn't going anywhere until I dealt with it. On some days, grief loomed over me, and I hunkered down. But on other days, I exploited grief as an ally and made it my very reason for finishing this book. I had to complete it! If it helped even one parent endure the tug-of-war between sadness and acceptance that grief had once imposed on me, I would see it through. Besides, I had heaven and earth on my side; I had heartifacts.

I first spoke publicly about my heart-shaped symbols of hope at the Children's Hospital of Pittsburgh in April of 2005. Prior to that, the unusual physical and spiritual phenomenon (which rounded the edges of my family's grieving) was a private affair. Then, by 2010, a dream inspired me to document my unorthodox antidote to grief. For some reason, I had been given heartifacts, and thus a gentler way of perceiving and enduring the loss of a child. Others needed to know.

To be honest, I feel a heavenly obligation to share the story inspired by my son, but I also approach the endeavor with extreme care. *I am not a grief expert; I am a grief survivor.* Firsthand experience has been my teacher, and the lessons I have learned are very organic, unadulterated. Grieving is work, and no parent is adequately prepared to bury their child. Thus *Heartifacts* is a book wrapped in prayers. I hope the words I have chosen are gentle (yet relatable) and compelling (but not burdensome). If you have lost a son or daughter, you have already been through enough. Your loss, like my own, defies quantification.

I have been cautious about bringing *Heartifacts* to the general public for another very specific reason. Portions of it were provided to me spiritually, and I was not prepared for that eventuality. (You will know those places when you read them.) Throughout those passages, I suspect I have documented inspiration from the spirit of my deceased son, God's Holy Spirit, or a blending of both. Honestly, I am not sure. What I am certain of is this: I have written from a sincere and humble heart. I never planned to become a speaker or an author—or an ambassador of hope for grieving parents. Life brought me to this juncture and filled my spirit with the following message: *it is possible for the human heart to heal from the most virulent grief imaginable.*

The death of any child is an insult to the human race; but for that child's parents, it creates a virtual wound that requires patience, gentleness, and a lifetime of management. A parent will never be the same after the loss of a child (and it is shortsighted to expect as much), but it is important that they believe they can heal from the trauma and—eventually—make peace with it. I assure you, no one wants to live with the depth of pain losing a child creates. Let me explain.

When Neil was born, I became a mother. His birth also marked my first experience of the distinctive love that a parent has for a child. It is an indelible love that is far beyond powerful; it is uncompromising. Such love connected Neil to me immediately. I was his, and he was mine…for all time. I will *never* forget that moment.

On the flip side, Neil's death rendered the inexplicable love I just described a dagger, and it pierced me to my core. My dream-come-true baby was gone, and the fact that he lived for nineteen years was of no consolation. During the early years of my bereavement for Neil, I felt trapped in a place I call *parent purgatory.* It was a haunting existence wherein I hovered between "the daily grind" and the promise of heaven. In other words, I was *here* and Neil was *there,* but my soul was somewhere in between. In those days, I knew my heart was beating, my feet were moving, and my face was emoting, but I also knew I was not as grounded or trusting as I had been before Neil's death. Losing him was a violation I feared I would never survive. But I have survived, and time has softened my perceptions; I now appreciate how lucky I was to accompany Neil on his life journey—all of it. It was a privilege to be his mother.

Thankfully, Neil died peacefully. (And he may have done so for my sake. He was that careful with me.) In return, I slipped into auto-grieving and accepted my lot as gracefully as any grieving mother could. About a month later, however, that all changed. Hitting an emotional and spiritual wall of grief was inevitable for me; even though I kept up a good front, my wanting for Neil was ceaseless. To address this, I finally called out to God—literally!

"How am I to go on?" I implored. "Neil is dead, my other kids are scared, and I am at a loss!"

Clearly, I needed a lifeline. My hope was shrinking, and my faith was wearing thin. God knew it, and I knew it.

Then, to my surprise, God answered my grief-saturated prayer almost instantly by replacing it with an indisputable, nature-made heart. The stone was clearly symbolic of love, but to me it also represented the hope I had all but lost. The new treasure assured me of two things: God was near, and death had not ended my relationship with my son. Death had transformed it.

Upon returning home, I had another awakening when I came across something Neil had created at least fifteen years prior. The discovery forced me to consider that there might be more to God's plan for my healing from grief than I had originally realized. (It also made every hair on my body rise up from the goose bumps I felt on my skin!) Without a doubt, Neil had never been shy about giving me hearts.

Image 1. Neil's heart art

Rediscovering this drawing by four-year-old Neil (so soon after receiving my first heartifact) made me wonder if my deceased son was in compassionate collusion with God! Together, they "rocked" my grieving world with hearts, symbolism perfectly reminiscent of Neil. From my perspective, none of the hearts were accidental; they were intentional—and I was astounded! Then another recollection about Neil pushed itself to the foreground. Eerily, it concerned something he had said to me just hours before his death.

"When this is over, Mom, I will find a way to help you," he whispered.

What Neil said took me aback; I never imagined that he could follow through with a promise like that! Instead, I acknowledged his valorous intentions with an affirmative nod. It was the best I could do. Speechless, I then swallowed hard and fought back tears.

My son's last words now seem to have been prophetic; Neil does help me since he died…*with hearts*! And, thanks to heartifacts, I have found my voice again.

In addition to presenting at the Children's Hospital of Pittsburgh, I have been a featured speaker for The American Cancer Society's Relay for Life and also during memorial gatherings at the Mercy Hospital of Pittsburgh, another division of the University of Pittsburgh Medical Center (UPMC). In the latter venue, I engage families who have suffered obstetrical losses, and it is especially difficult. Thankfully, the heartifacts, which support the story, seem to open the door to hope for even the saddest of the sad.

Everyone who loves anyone will someday grieve, and each will do so uniquely. I share my journey with one hope only: that you will be encouraged by it. The truth is *all of our children are engaged in a timeless, boundless journey of love, not death*. I will show you…

heart by heart by heart.

ONE

DREAM 2010: THE LAY OF THE LAND

*I*n my dream, *I am looking at the desk in my office and remembering when it was an orderly work space—one at which I had always been productive. But now I see it is sagging dismally under the weight of enormous stacks of paper and folders.*

"What happened here?" I wonder.

Then I am stricken with a new awareness—a night terror. The overloaded desk is burdened not with paper, but with the pieces of my own disheveled life!

From July of 1998 until 2010, when I had the dream, my actual life had taken a course toward something I barely recognized. This dream included a true picture of my desk by the end of that time period—distorted and exaggerated, but accurate. The helter-skelter piles of paper on top of it had grown like stalagmites during the previous twelve years, and my former life of continuity and cohesion had become one of addressing issues in order of their emergency status.

One particular decision marked the beginning of the catastrophic period that seized my family. I am still amazed that any of my children and I survived the onslaught.

The 1998 crisis occurred just days before my fortieth birthday. That was when I learned my husband had set his sights on a new life—and it did not include me. After being together for twenty-three years, his decision rattled my world like an earthquake. We had always been an amicable couple who had no history of discord. For these reasons, I did not register my husband's changing heart before it fully morphed away from me. I felt ambushed.

Upon further examination, I wondered if I had been too focused on and driven by my own responsibilities to notice my husband's disconnect. I was an "all-in" full-time homemaker and mother of four active children. One thing is certain; I could not have been any other kind of mother.

Our family had distinct challenges, but we were a good family, a team. Or so I thought. I had never considered a life without my husband in it, until I tripped over the new design he had adopted for his own future. This revelation was beyond painful for me, mostly because I considered him to be completely trustworthy. Out of nowhere, a sudden and gargantuan void developed between us, so expansive and deep that I thought I might fall into it and die. I did my best to avoid the abyss and carry on, but my heart wept for years.

My four children, Neil, Davin, Lauren, and Gregory, were careful with me and loved me through the trauma of this unsettling turn of events. But they were powerless when it came to forestalling the disappointment and disillusionment that infiltrated our home. The new atmosphere under our roof was suffocating, and tiptoeing through the rubble of our previous family life was devastating to the kids and me. Thus we operated in a state of confusion and shocked disbelief, while trying to minimize any aftershocks from this cataclysm.

I agreed to an in-house marital separation for seven months, but privately I prayed that the horrific nightmare would cease. I wanted my family back. Not long into the arrangement, it became all too clear to me: that was never going to happen. I was flying solo in a home that felt like a wax museum. The children and I were present in form, but our essences were on guard, stifled, as if lodged deep within paraffin look-alikes. The diplomatic separation was farcical, freakish, and bizarre.

Dad coming home with the aura of a single man was baffling to my children, but for me, it was demoralizing. I watched him leave the house (spit-shined and refreshed) day after day, week after week, and month after month. The charade had to end. The longer our mock separation continued, the more disposable I felt. Worse yet, it modeled something I would never want any of my children to replicate. What began as a lousy idea ended up being a pathetic mess, and I needed to reconcile myself to a life I had never imagined: a life without the father of my children.

After a complete physical separation of our households, I was left to mend my shredded self-esteem, restore some stability at home, and patch a family life together for my children and me. To reinforce my new (necessary) goals, I reminded myself that home was certainly no place for smoke and mirrors or hidden agendas. My children deserved better. I deserved better.

The children and I were deeply saddened over the dissolution of our original family, a group once committed to meeting its challenges with each member's loyalty and support. We also missed the traditions and closeness we used to share. In spite of any hurdles we faced, I *never* doubted our family's ability to overcome anything, as long as we stuck together. It was hard to accept the death of such a family, so I tried to reason my way through what had happened.

My husband and I were both dedicated and diligent people. We might have been attacking life from different rails (he on a career one and I on a homemaker one), but I always believed we were moving along the right track for the right reasons. When I learned that we were not moving in the same direction, as you already know, the news derailed me.

The ties between our rails, our kids, were adorable and lively. They made us laugh, they made us cry, and I think it is safe to assume that their father still loves each of them as much as I do. Despite the ten-year age span between our oldest and youngest, our four kids were a close-knit brood. They had the usual sibling differences, but few. My kids cavorted with, protected, and rallied one another on. Over time, they even developed a comical language of their own. For example, Greg was Gerg, Lauren was Nerual, Davin was Nivad and Neil was Lien. Like the Pied Piper, Neil started the trend, and the little ones were happy to follow along.

Once becoming victims of a fractured marriage, my children changed. Their creative and carefree spirits became anything but carefree in the wake of the disaster. They were no longer sure of how to act or what to believe in. In a nutshell, the effects of the abandoned marriage magnified every other challenge life brought forth for my family—and life brought forth plenty of them.

As 1999 got under way, my children and I were straining to see any bright spots in the cloud that rested over our fragmented family. Thankfully, Neil's graduation from high school and acceptance into college gave us two positive things upon which to focus (especially since his school career had been exceptional and his future was as promising as anyone's). Preparing to celebrate Neil's noteworthy milestones was a healthy distraction for the crew at home. Shockingly, however, Neil's optimistic future was in jeopardy by midsummer. Something besides a marital breakdown had been festering indefinitely, and it was even more hidden and more horrible.

By July of 1999, Neil was diagnosed with a rare and unforgiving pediatric bone cancer called Ewing's sarcoma. We learned this fact only five weeks after his June graduation from Mt. Lebanon High School. Suddenly, the marital separation seemed trivial. Everything else seemed trivial! Neil's health needs quickly moved to front and center, and so did a daunting treatment protocol. To make matters worse, his beckoning college life imploded before his very eyes. It was hard to accept that my injured family was under siege again. This time was so much worse, though; our sweet Neil was the new target, and his life hung in the balance. The hideous news broke the hearts of everyone who knew him.

Our family's contorted reality became even more painful, exhausting, and bewildering after Neil's diagnosis of cancer, but that did not prevent his natural yet subtle leadership qualities from rising to the top. Neil was deeply grounded, and he set the emotional and mental pace for the medical marathon ahead. We all fell in line and supported his determination to beat cancer, but something more was apparent to me; Neil was fighting to preserve what was left of our family. Neil was loyal...true blue.

Neil's siblings and I followed his lead and kept our tears to ourselves (as best we could). No one wanted to add to his distress, especially as he faced the life-threatening monster called Ewing's. Anchored among his family, friends, and home, on a sea of quietly persistent faith in God, my eighteen-year-old bravely faced his uncertain horizon with hope.

Neil withstood the first ten months of aggressive medical treatment and was rewarded with a cancer-free body scan in June of 2000. We celebrated this wonderful pronouncement, but unfortunately, other bad news had surfaced in the interim. My mother had been diagnosed with colon cancer four months prior, on Saint Valentine's Day, and her odds of survival were grim. To make matters worse, we also learned that one of my sisters-in-law was battling invasive breast cancer at around the same time. The terror inflicted upon my extended family during that time period was unbelievable.

As you can see, the start of the highly anticipated New Millennium was rough on the Horgan clan. While other families around the world ushered in 2000 as a fresh start, ours was supporting three family members who were fighting for their lives. Neil's good news in June gave us all cause to hope for the best, however. Despite statistics, we prayed that my mother and my sister-in-law would be blessed with successful outcomes, too.

Sadly, cancer took my mother, Evelyn Murray Horgan, only six months after her diagnosis. She died on August 15, 2000, the annual feast day of the Assumption of the Blessed Mother of Jesus. For Catholics, that date commemorates Mary's bypassing death and being assumed into heaven, body and soul. Many members of my family noted the coincidental date and found solace in our own mother leaving her mortal life behind on the Blessed Mother's holy day (especially since Evelyn had been quietly devoted to Mary throughout her life). In an odd way, the date seemed fitting for my mother's passing, even auspicious. Like Mary, Evelyn possessed a heavenly balance of strength and gentleness. And both women gave life their all.

With my father by her side, Evelyn made her way through her adult life humbly, sincerely, and with depth. She brought forth eleven children who loved her, knew the richness of family life, and appreciated the power of commitment. My father, a well-educated and affable man, considered my mother to be his rock. In truth, Evelyn was everyone's rock! The steady drumbeat of her life said all that needed to be said about Evelyn. Moreover, it was a reflection of the confidence she had in God. My mother calmly trusted Him with faith that was truly Marian.

The day of Evelyn's actual burial was a solemn one for the entire Horgan family, but for Neil and me, it turned out to be confounding. That is because August 19, 2000, was also the date of Neil's (belated) first day of college. Talk about mixed emotions! The word "torn" does not begin to describe how Neil and I felt as we left Grandma's wake, packed the car, and then drove to University Park; it was surreal.

Neil and I forced ourselves to celebrate each mile along the way to Penn State University that day, despite our dueling emotions. Attending PSU had always been a dream of Neil's, but being on his way after successfully battling cancer made it all the more meaningful. The miles we tallied represented his triumph over each heinous medical assault he had overcome during the previous year. In fact, the farther we got from Pittsburgh, the lighter my victorious son and I felt. Instead of lamenting my mother's death, Neil and I made our way to Happy Valley as if Grandma were right there with us.

"She has to be!" we exclaimed. Neil had earned his good health, he was back on course, and he was reclaiming his life.

Certainly heaven was celebrating, too!

One thing that *never* crossed our minds on that pivotal August day was that Neil's university experience was to last only three months. By Thanksgiving break, in November of 2000, his long-awaited college life was over. Ewing's sarcoma had taken hold of him again, and with even more vengeance this time. Neil fought on but died on the other side of winter, just seven months after getting settled in at Penn State University. Losing him was unfathomable.

Years later, I was surprised by something I had not realized about the timing of Neil's death; like Grandma Horgan, he crossed over from this life on a holy day that seemed divinely fitting for him. It was March 19, the annual feast day of St. Joseph the Carpenter. He was the Blessed Mother's husband and Jesus Christ's earthly father.

To me, there was an uncanny coincidence about Neil's new life beginning on that particular day: St. Joseph and Neil were both woodworkers (as was Jesus). Relatively few people knew this about Neil. Remarks that he was friendly, handsome, athletic, and bright were common (and are sincerely appreciated to this day), but only one person ever told me he was a natural at woodworking. I learned the latter from his shop teacher during an annual high school open house. Neil, who had come to this instructor with no knowledge of carpentry, demonstrated promise with the art from the beginning.

Taking woodshop was a detour for Neil—a diversion from his text-laden academic curriculum. Even so, he took the course serious-ly: his teacher's remarks and the quality of the projects Neil brought home told me so. Each one revealed his developing acumen for the craft, along with his creativity, patience, and introspective nature.

Woodworking turned out to be a perfect expressive outlet for my quiet, multifaceted guy.

Neil completed one particularly meaningful woodshop project toward the end of his junior year. It was a *heart-shaped* music box, and he had carved it out of a single block of solid cherry, a hardwood. When he first presented the heart to me, I was overwhelmed (as any mother would have been). First of all, I had no idea of the woodworking talent he possessed. Secondly, it was evident that Neil had put a lot of time and thought into what he placed upon my hands that day. The gorgeous wooden creation was remarkable in every way. And if a gift ever screamed *I love you*, this one did. I could hardly express my appreciation to him. Seeing that my emotions were about to unravel, Neil gently interrupted the moment and reached for the heart.

"Just for a moment," was all he said.

When I extended the carved box back toward him, he accepted it, wound a brass key on its underside (something I had not yet noticed) and then returned it to me. Once it was safely resting upon my palms again, he carefully removed the lid. That was when "Music of the Night," a nostalgic song from *The Phantom of the Opera*, began playing. If I had not been at a loss for words before, I definitely was by then! In silence, I absorbed the love-infused gift from Neil and appreciated how very, very blessed I was.

Image 2. Neil's handcrafted wooden heart box (May 1998)

In retrospect, Neil's choice to create a heart for me in 1998 was another foretelling decision. He had not been assigned to make a heart-shaped anything in woodshop; he had chosen to. I later learned that it was one of many options that his teacher had presented to the class.

My reaction to Neil's one-of-a-kind gift triggered an expression of humble satisfaction from him that remains with me. It was a perfect moment in time for both of us. Unfortunately, it bore no resemblance to the months that soon followed.

Neither Neil nor I could have known that the purity and innocence of our exchange in 1998 would be overshadowed by divorce and disease during 1999. Both moved in to loom over our family until April of 2001, when the first heartifact found me. That moment confirmed the true value of all the hearts Neil had ever given to me previously; each is now more than priceless. That was also the day that heart stones came to represent a supernatural continuation of Neil's pattern of expressing love. Their message to me was so simple and so clear: despite death, Neil had found his way to love on. Not only that, he had made sure I would recognize it!

Losing my mother and my son to cancer within seven months was numbing for me and my entire family. But there is good news to report: my sister-in-law still graces our lives. She survived breast cancer and is an elegant inspiration to a very grateful family.

When I reflect upon that profoundly insane time period, I must tell you one more thing: I am not the only one who feels that my mother's physical demise was mysteriously sudden. In fact, considering the role she played in Neil's life as it came to a close, her passing seemed to be another curiously providential event. Some of us even wonder if God was looking out for Neil by calling Evelyn home first. You might agree, once considering another revelation Neil presented to me as he prepared to make his transition from this life to the next.

At the time, Neil gently said to me, "Mom, will you be all right if I just fall asleep now? I mean, if you will be all right, I am ready."

Barely digesting this, I replied, "You know me, Neil. I will be 'all right.'"

But inside my head, I was not convinced of this at all. My thoughts were reeling.

Then he said, "Grandma is waiting."

I was stunned!

Silently processing this, I thought, "Oh my goodness! Is Neil telling me that my mother is here to accompany him on his journey?"

I did not question him directly, however; by then Neil was exhausted, and his being at peace was all that mattered to me. Besides, I was always on board for Neil (honestly, he never gave me a reason to be otherwise). If that now meant letting him go, I was not going to hold him back. What he told me about his grandmother waiting for him helped me to be brave for his sake, too; it reassured me that hope would carry Neil beyond his dying. How lovely that it manifested as my mother.

As you can see, the little things Neil said to me during the last twenty-four hours of his life were anything but little. Every last gem he offered was written upon my heart, and all of them have been etched there ever since. In a way, I have preserved Neil's last words just as I have preserved the kitchen table "heart art" he drew when he was four. I guess it's a mom thing.

As dawn crested on March 19, 2001, Neil was no longer conscious. He was resting and finally comfortable. I was stalwart and vigilant in his honor, but inside, I was as fragile as a snowflake in June. It was hard to for me to believe that our conversations were really over. It seemed that all I could do was observe each precious breath he took through the blur of my silent tears. By morning, the world was opaque to me.

Then it happened.

Neil's breathing stopped.

And time stood still.

Very still.

But a moment later, sunlight streamed into Neil's room, and I felt his freedom. That, combined with what Neil had told me about my mother, enabled me to take my own next breath. I thanked God for providing heaven and a loving grandmother for my beautiful son. At least one of us would be free of pain, disappointment, and sadness.

Conversely, the lay of the land in my life reflected the impact of three distinct traumas: my marital breakup, my mother's death, and the absence of Neil. These losses layered themselves upon me and infiltrated every thought I claimed, both conscious and unconscious. My mind never rested as I tried to make sense of my teetering and convoluted new reality.

As I considered the unstable paper stacks on the desk in my dream, a shiny red apple popped into view. Quickly, I realized that it was not edible, but it was surely beautiful…like a jewel. The decorative apple was snugly wedged between two document piles on the congested desktop. I considered prying it loose, but worried that I might instigate an avalanche of papers and make matters worse. Even so, its crimson enamel finish drew me closer. Then I noticed the apple's sturdy stem and vibrant green leaf. Finally, I wondered if the elegant fruit had a function.

"That apple looks substantial," my dreaming self thought. "Maybe it's a paperweight."

Curiously, I reached for it. But the apple vanished before I could grab it.

(Of course it did! Dreams are like that.)

Then, from behind me, a massive, sculpted right arm reached over my right shoulder. It belonged to a man whose moves were slow and deliberate. There was something in his hand, too, I could tell; his closed fist was wrapped around some kind of orb. After another dream moment, he released his grip around the object, and there was the apple that had just disappeared from my desk! It was now sitting on the unknown man's open palm. I was fascinated, and for some reason not fearful of the stranger behind me.

"Who is the mysterious being attached to the arm before me, and why is he presenting this faux fruit to me?" I asked myself.

The larger-than-life forearm then manipulated the hand attached to it and turned the apple over as gracefully as a major league pitcher positioning his fingers on a baseball. Finally, the purpose of the peculiar apple was revealed to me; it was a pencil sharpener!

I awoke with a start just then. I strained to recall every detail of the vision my subconscious had created while I slept. The dream of my congested work space tried to escape my memory, but my intellect chased after it ruthlessly. I grabbed a pen and notebook from my bedside table and captured what I could.

"What could such a dream possibly mean?" I mused, as I scribbled some notes.

Left to my own analysis, I pondered the distinct images of my dream long after I had awoken. There seemed to be some significant symbolism in it: heavy and disheveled piles of paper, a pencil sharpener, the right arm of a man enlightening me…instructing me…guiding me, and an apple. Truthfully, interpreting this obscure dream presented less of a challenge than comprehending my real life!

I could figure this one out. I was sure of it.

Clearly, I needed to deal with my papers (my recent history). To my awake self, the unwieldy stacks in my dream represented my life after the fall of my family—a life from which I desperately wanted to run. Instead, the authoritative man with the pencil sharpener suggested that I needed to do some documenting. The message was a daunting one; I did not want to go through any of what had happened to my family again. There had to be an alternative reason for me to write. All of a sudden, I had a pretty good idea of what it was.

"Okay," I thought. "I will sharpen my pencil. I will write."

Then my conscious self wondered, "Who could possibly be offering the pencil sharpener to me?"

Was that Neil's pitching arm extended before me, exaggerated in every way by my subconscious? Heaven knows I had seen him throw plenty of baseballs. Or could it have been God's own powerful right arm, as it is depicted on the ceiling of the Sistine Chapel in Michelangelo's *Creation of Adam* painting? Ironically, the arm I saw in my dream contained attributes I could relate to both Neil and God.

I felt the apple's meaning was obvious. Apples have symbolized knowledge and teaching for as long as I can remember.

"But if that is so," I asked myself, "what is the knowledge to be shared, and who is doing the teaching?"

"Am I being taught, or am I to teach?" I wondered.

Whatever its meaning, I felt compelled to pay close attention to that particular dream. Someone, or something, seemed to be telling me, "Get to writing, Maggie!"

With no certain answers to my questions, I gave up trying to analyze my dream and decided to follow my intuition instead. The unusual vignette provided by my subconscious told me to write, so I began composing the manuscript for *Heartifacts* that very day. I did not approach the task as a trained writer, however. I approached it as someone who had a message to deliver. I knew I would need guidance along the way, and I trusted that it would emerge during the process. Whatever needed to be recorded would be recorded. Whatever lessons were to be imparted would be imparted. In any case, I have done my best to follow my guidance and bring forth a book worthy of your attention.

TWO

THE REQUEST, 2005

How to begin? Where to start? What to leave in? What to omit? These questions arose long before my dream of 2010. I first wrestled with them in 2005, when I was asked to share my wounded family's story of recovery from grief. The seeds of the initial request were planted on a nondescript afternoon in March of that year. I remember the day well. Another Pittsburgh winter was giving way to springtime.

Energized by the changing seasons, my three children and I were out and about like other Pittsburghers emerging from hibernation. Midday, we stopped for lunch inside the food court of our local mall, South Hills Village. The place was like an airport terminal; people were coming and going as though late for their next connection. While traversing the hub, I recognized Reverend Richard Freeman, who was heading in our direction. As his gaze skimmed above us, I took a deep breath; I was not *at all* sure I wanted him to notice us.

Ambivalence churned in the pit of my stomach about a reunion with the reverend—even an innocuous one in a food court. Could my heart take it? Would I come undone? Would reintroducing him to Greg, Davin, and Lauren upset their carefree day, considering the nature of his previous association with our family? Their last memory of Richard Freeman, like mine, was connected with their older brother's terminal illness. Seeing him triggered my own flashback to those uneasy times.

Reverend Freeman was one of my first new acquaintances after learning of Neil's cancer diagnosis on July 20, 1999. He has since become the managing pastoral care director at the Children's Hospital of Pittsburgh. I met him during Neil's first inpatient stay at Children's. His job was to provide spiritual and emotional support to patients and families facing the most challenging of childhood medical situations.

Richard Freeman was hard to miss—especially in the halls of a children's hospital. At first glance, I was struck by his stature; he was a towering man who looked like a professional athlete. But there was something more about him that I could not help but notice: his countenance and warm smile were arresting. As scared as I was to be in an oncology department with one of my own children, I felt a certain security in Reverend Freeman's company.

Neil also met Richard Freeman on the same day, and the two connected. My son and I both felt a little safer with the reverend in our strange new world. Let's face it—Neil and I had just landed on Planet Cancer, and we were foreigners. We felt our confused and broken hearts could rest a bit in Pastor Freeman's care. When the three of us first met, he had been an island of relief for Neil and me. Sadly, the rest of our world had been spinning wickedly out of control back then.

My three surviving children and I were still learning to ambulate among the rest of humanity when I spotted our old friend in the mall. Navigating about our community, with grief as our ill-fitting accessory, often left the kids and me feeling like strangers in our own backyard. Relating to people who were going about their ordinary lives had become challenging to us. We could no longer relate to "ordinary." Neil had been so central to our lives that even going out for a bite to eat could be stress-inducing, especially if we ran into anyone who knew our history. Even though years had passed, our being recognized by Reverend Freeman seemed to have the same worrisome potential. I waited to see how things would unfold.

A moment later, Richard caught sight of us in the bustling food court. When he and I made eye contact, we smiled and waved at each other across the distance. I froze momentarily, but he did not. He started moving in our direction without hesitation.

"Heads up!" I briefed the kids. "Reverend Freeman, from Children's Hospital, is headed our way."

We all instinctively braced our vulnerable selves, but soon found that our anxiety was unwarranted. Reverend Freeman's greeting was deeply compassionate and respectful. He was already sensitized to the complexity of our journey.

"What a relief!" I thought.

No awkward updates or explanations would be required of us. Consequently, any angst we harbored about our chance encounter with him dissipated promptly. Freeman dealt with fragile families every day, and it showed. Just as before, we were handled with care.

Our exchange in the food court was pleasant and brief, but also genuine. Reverend Freeman always led with his heart. When he walked away, however, something in his glance (or in the nod of his head) led me to believe that I would hear from him in the near future.

I even recall whispering to my daughter, "Pastor Freeman has something on his mind, Lauren. I'm not sure what it is, but he will be in touch."

Sure enough, I received a call from him a few weeks later.

"Maggie, this is Reverend Freeman," I heard him say, in his characteristically calm and soothing manner.

After I replied to his greeting, he got to the point of his call. He had a request.

"Maggie, I am a member of the Memorial Service Planning Committee here at Children's, and we have a favor to ask of you. We are searching for a parent who has survived the loss of a child and is willing to assist us in comforting our newly grieving families. We need someone with whom the grieving can specifically relate…someone whose encouragement will be meaningful to them."

Twice yearly, Children's Hospital of Pittsburgh offers a service of remembrance for families of patients who have died. This is not true of all hospitals, not even all children's hospitals. Pittsburgh's pediatric hospital has chosen to provide these opportunities for grieving families, even though no one likes to draw attention to the fact that children sometimes die. It is a brave and progressive move, one that I respect.

Grieving parents are a fragile lot, a lonely lot. By bringing them together to share their individual losses, perhaps participants can find a place of belonging. It is not a community that any parent looks forward to joining, but only another grieving parent can really relate to a person who has lost a child. This truth had been brought to the attention of the Memorial Service Planning Committee at Children's through parent feedback surveys from prior services. Such feedback prompted Reverend Freeman's call to me.

As he put it, "Surviving parents definitely appreciate our remembering their children with a memorial service, but they also question our ability to truly relate to their losses, Maggie. As many parents have pointed out to us, we on the committee have not walked in their shoes."

He then commented on how well my children and I appeared to be when he spoke to us at the mall. To him, we looked as though we had successfully survived Neil's passing and the ensuing grief. This impressed Reverend Freeman, and he wondered how we had done it.

He specifically asked, "How did the four of you achieve the wholeness I observed when I last saw you?"

To which I exclaimed incredulously (to myself), "Really? We appeared to be whole?"

I was happy to hear that my surviving children and I looked as if we had weathered the road to recovery from grief, but it sure had been a long and winding trail. Even so, I agreed to examine our journey and figure out what had helped us along. The least I could do was find an honest, thoughtful answer to his query.

Reverend Freeman then explained how the memorial services had evolved since the one I had attended for Neil in 2002. At that time, they were held monthly and relatively few families attended each service. By 2005, the services were being held semiannually and the crowd at each gathering was much larger. If I agreed to help with the upcoming service, it would be as a speaker addressing an auditorium full of grieving parents and caregivers. It would be my job to share some firsthand wisdom about coping with grief after the loss of a child.

The reverend's request took me by surprise.

Nervously, I admitted to him, "I have not delivered a speech of any consequence since high school student-council elections in 1976!" And that experience was trivial, compared to the audience and topic he proposed I address; those presented new and distinct challenges.

"But at least my candidate won!" I added, then blurted out, "Oh, and I almost forgot—I also took a public speaking course as a freshman at Penn State!"

The latter fact made me no more qualified to address a forum of grieving parents than my high school speech did, but my desire to help had become obvious to Reverend Freeman. He also knew my nerves were responding as I tried to convince myself that I was comfortable with public speaking. He knew just how to neutralize my anxiety about speaking.

With a chuckle, a sigh, and a reflective pause, he assured me, "You are more than qualified, Maggie. You have walked *many* miles in a grieving parent's moccasins."

He knew my grief was complicated. He also knew how much of it I had borne alone. I think he also suspected that, however my kids and I had adapted, it was not by skimming the surface of the difficult issue.

By the end of the call, I had agreed to speak at the next memorial service. I had one month to prepare, but no clue where to start. I only knew that I wanted to bring a measure of comfort to the heartbroken strangers in my audience. If I could do *anything* to ease the inexorable pain of another family going through the kind of loss mine had, I would try. The weeks slipped by too quickly as I struggled to write my speech. There were only two things I was sure of as I wrestled with my thoughts: children had perished, and their families were in severe pain. From my perspective, those realities alone created a solemn bond between me and my future audience, my new brethren.

So many questions emerged as I attempted to get ready for the memorial service: What had each child been like? What had led to each child's passing? How many of the children had died suddenly? How many after a prolonged illness? Had they ever known good health (as Neil once had, prior to his diagnosis)? What were the ages of the children being remembered? What were the parents like? Did they have other children? How could I reach younger audience members grieving for their siblings? How could I comfort a grandparent's double-dip grief for both their grandchild and their own child (who had become their grieving child)? What were each family's spiritual moorings? Did everyone attending believe in God? What were their notions about an afterlife? Did they believe heaven exists? Was their own healing something they believed was possible? Did the newly bereaved I would face have any hope left at all?

Truthfully, all bets are off when it comes to predicting how those surviving a child's death will cope. It is a circumstance that compromises even closely held beliefs and, for better or worse, realigns priorities. Had I bitten off more than I could chew by agreeing to share with such a wounded group of people? My soul-searching continued, regardless. I was determined to deliver something reassuring and positive during the memorial service.

Still unsure of what would be the right message to bring, I turned to Reverend Freeman for advice (or, at least, helpful suggestions) just two weeks before the memorial gathering.

With confidence, he replied, "Maggie, you will know exactly what to say."

My heart interpreted his comment to mean, "Say what we cannot."

Within one week of the memorial service, I was still at a loss for words! So, with no one else to turn to and no time to waste, I sat before my keyboard and began typing a letter. There was someone I had always been able to confide in, and count on, in the past. Maybe he could help me get started.

I typed:

> *Dear Neil,*
> *What should I tell a room full of parents like me?*

What followed took me by complete surprise; I got the direction I sought!

THREE

THE COMPASS

Keep it simple, Mom. You know what it's like—the terror, the horror, the vast vacancy left in your heart after burying a child. Other families need to know what only you can share with them. They need to see what only you can show them. I know surviving me was not a job you ever wanted, but you accepted it. You had no choice but to accept it. On March 19, 2001, it was my time to go. That's all, Mom. It was just my time.

Of course, I didn't want to move on any more than you wanted to release me. During the preceding months, however, you and I had both come to realize nobody was leaving anybody...not really. We are, and have always been, intrinsically connected.

Even before my physical birth on June 30, 1981, I sense you knew me, Mom. Regardless of space and time, the connection between us has always been one of love, a manifestation of the divine spirit we have in common. By the way, that is how a full life is truly measured, Mom...in love, not years. According to that quantifier, *my life was, and remains, full to the brim. My ultimate physical absence, the illusion called death, is only that, Mom...an illusion.*

Regardless, through the journey we shared, you know the monster that brought us to total dread and the beastly pain of grieving for a child. If you could spare anyone the same, I know you would. Perhaps you can assist those families with what you and I have learned with absolute certainty: the spirits of children (and other loved ones) who have died do not leave. Please tell the bereaved, those of us who have passed on have been, and always will be, connected to those we love. What binds us together is infinite; it is love itself.

Our bodies were the vehicles God provided to carry our spirits during our earthly existence. Everyone's body has an expiration date, but our spirits never expire. It is a human prerogative to accept or reject this. God-given free will gives spirits, ambulating as humans, the final say about how they interpret all of their earthly experiences, including death. But there is only one accurate interpretation from this side of the veil: our limitless spirits are very much alive over here—in fact, they are liberated! Death is a nonspiritual, physical separation...a mortal phenomenon. Love is our true self, and it is a spiritual existence. Mortality has no power over love, and the Holy Spirit will always support connections of love.

I can see how grief becomes the ultimate challenge for loving human beings, though. Clearly, grieving is hard work, and grieving for a child is likely the hardest. You can attest to that, Mom. Heaven understands this and wants to support those who are grieving—especially families of young ones whose lives have run their course. Our bodies were not eternal, but our spirits sure are. Love, the essence of the Holy Spirit, is parceled to all human beings. It does not leave when someone dies, but it may be hard to recognize through the tears and anguish of grief. Love is not confined to any form, either. It is free. Your heart recognizes love. My heart does, too. All hearts can recognize and engage love that is everlasting, but they must choose to.

I know this is hard for you, Mom. But I have no way of knowing how hard, since I never had to watch a child go. The good news is that neither you nor I have to exist without the other. I know you know this. You sense my nearness in so many ways, like when you are having a particularly sad day and every hair on your body stands on end when you think of me. I am there, wrapping you in love. Or when a special memory of time we shared when I was growing up makes your heart race with joy. I am there. Sometimes you even get goose bumps when you think of me (here, we call them angel bumps). I know this because I am with you then, too.

The earthly life we shared certainly wasn't easy, Mom, but it was rich. Even on the day my doctors told us there was no way my body could defeat the disease it was fighting, we got through it together. When we heard the news we never thought we'd hear, it was devastating to both of us. And the minute we were left alone with that information, we cried. But when I was finally able to speak, I remember saying, "I don't want to leave you, Mom."

Without the slightest hesitation, you replied, "Nobody's leaving anybody. We will never be apart, Neil."

How did you know, Mom? Or did you know? Whatever the case, that dialogue instigated our pledge to remain connected no matter what transpired. Well, here we are, keeping our promise— and I know I am freaking you out with this information!

Besides feeling those goose bumps you feel right now, Mom, do you realize you are also drenching your keyboard? You know, that cannot be good.

Just remember, though you are there, and I am here, we are divinely connected for all time. That's the way it is between parents and their children who have died. By the way, I am all about watching out for Davin, Lauren, and Greg—and they know it. Brothers and sisters get special attention from heaven when they lose a sibling.

What I share is true and the bereaved must be reassured of it, Mom. Tell them how you know. Tell those who grieve about our heart stones…the ones you call heartifacts.

Are you serious, Neil? Tell them about heartifacts? They will think I am crazy and more steeped in grief than I even realize. Maybe I am! Yet I believe you are absolutely right. Maybe I should introduce our heartifacts to parents who grieve. But before I do, Neil, there is something I need to know; how was it that you were so much better at accepting your new life than I have been at accepting it? I realize you had no choice, but let me explain why I ask.

You never seemed to get "stuck" on the villainous plan life ended up having for you, yet I still struggle with memories of it. (What parent wouldn't?) Not only that, I also seem to scourge myself with musings about our "normal" years together, as members of a cohesive family. From the time you were born, there was something magical about our relationship. How will I ever get from those feelings to the task at hand? It is so overwhelming.

And I am drenching my poor keyboard again.

Gee, Neil, this is rough.

Seriously, though, how did you do it? I mean, I watched you go through the greatest of pain and the cruelest of indignities while fighting for your life, yet you never complained. First, there were five or six weeklong cycles of chemotherapy, and you received one every four weeks. The goal of those interventions was to shrink the grapefruit-sized tumor buried in your chest. The smaller it got, the more safely it could be removed. The deadly menace was never visible externally; it was attached to the interior side of your breast bone and nestled between your heart and lungs. Even miniaturized, just getting to it was life-threatening and required extremely radical thoracic surgery starting with a chest wall resection. Then, after successfully removing the

Ewing's tumor, the master surgeon rebuilt your ribcage and anchored it to a bionic sternum.

Those extensive procedures took most of a day, but you withstood them. In barely a month, you were fully recovered—and to celebrate this, you snuck up to Seven Springs for an afternoon of skiing with your closest friends! You had to: it was never the "right" time to for you to rest on your laurels. Every time you got to feeling good again, it was time for the next agonizing intervention. Battling ever-ominous Ewing's sarcoma was a full time job. Never mind holidays, too; preparation for your stem cell transplant began on Christmas Eve, 1999. By New Year's Eve, a week later, your immune system was completely wiped out. The good news about that was your body had survived being prepared to receive the stem cells that had been harvested from you shortly after your diagnosis. At the time, we were forewarned: a stem cell transplant was a long shot, but it was your best shot at a full and lasting recovery from the malicious bone cancer.

In one doctor's words, "What a patient goes through in preparation for a stem cell transplant is probably more painful than death itself."

Disconcerting as this statement was, the alternative of not trying for a complete cure was bleaker. As predicted, the transplant preparation was painful and it did bring you to the edge of life, but you persisted. Yes, you made it through…just in time for a few months of radiation to your chest (and every vital organ in the vicinity). Despite it all, Ewing's sarcoma returned within six months of your cancer-free (June 2000) body scan. And when it did, your doctors were out of ammunition.

It took twenty months for Ewing's sarcoma to land its final blow, but you never backed down from the demon. Through it all, you remained Neil: courageous, optimistic, and kind. My heart still aches when I recall these details, Neil. It truly is almost too much to bear.

Observing and supporting you through all of it gave me a glimpse into how you approached every medical challenge you faced.

In hindsight, an attitude of resolve was your armor. Whenever you needed to be hospitalized, you reached for your beaten-up "Just Do It" T-shirt.

"It's a classic!" you'd proclaim as you wriggled into it (holes and all).

The popular, no-nonsense directive from Nike was emblazoned across your chest each time you went to task against the unspeakable. Upon reflection, I realize the corporate slogan had become your unspoken mantra.

I now see that the same mantra is about to become my new directive, for you passed a heavenly baton to me when I held my first heartifact. Somehow, with God's support, you knew exactly what I needed when engaging hope became too hard for me. That is why I now intend to pronounce our heart-filled message to as many grieving families as I can reach. And I will do so with the greatest care and reverence; I cannot help but believe what you and I have to share is holy, God-driven. I am forever grateful for the hope-laden "batons" that have streamed into my life since you passed, Neil. To me the hearts are miraculous, and all of heaven has my pledge: I will "Just Do It" for folk like me...with heartifacts.

FOUR

THE DISCOVERY

Neil was eighteen, had just graduated from high school, and was looking forward to college when he was diagnosed with the aggressive bone cancer called Ewing's sarcoma. The treatment protocol prescribed to Neil had been equally aggressive; but, in his case, it was no match for the rare condition. About a year and a half later, Neil's body became too depleted to host the war that had been waging on inside it any longer. Completely exhausted, he asked for my blessing upon sleep he could no longer stave off.

"I am just so tired, Mom. Will you be all right...if I...just go to sleep?" Neil whispered.

I disguised my disbelief that the moment of his death was at hand and assured him, "I will be all right, if you will be all right, Neil. I only ask that you do one thing: when you see that white light everyone talks about, *charge straight through it*...and never look back. Then, I will be all right."

A short while later, I believe Neil did just that. It was March 19, 2001. And a dozen years later, here I am...being all right.

Things have not been particularly easy since that fateful day, but I have always done my best to adhere to the promise I made to Neil. I have gotten up *every* morning since then (whether I wanted to or not), my other children have reached adulthood *mostly* intact (a work in progress), and I have never abandoned hope that life still has merit (though for years it was debatable). For a while, those were the variables that constituted "being all right" for me. I thank God that my outlook improved over time. Eventually, I got back to being more happy than sad. But believe me, there had been times when I wondered if I ever would.

When I first lost Neil, there were few people with whom I could relate. As years and events presented themselves, however, I found respite among other grieving parents, my compatriots. With them, I felt a spontaneous and precious kinship. Among them, I found a place where my grieving self was understood, allowed. Perhaps the void in one grieving parent's heart can harbor another's pain for just a little while. Sometimes I think that may be all such a parent needs to make it to the next level of healing.

The weight of grieving for my own son accompanied everything I did, in the beginning. Even the simplest of tasks felt insurmountable. When this new strain of grief imposed itself upon my already-gnarled life, I felt as if I had been airdropped into a foggy, puzzling labyrinth. Groping and stumbling through the haunting maze made my days seem endless. What was most frightening, though, were the moments when I did not want to bother at all.

"What is the point?" I would ask myself.

I was not used to feeling helpless.

Since those days, I have been assured that the defeatist thoughts that sometimes haunted me back then were a normal reaction to what I had been through. It is a common theme for many grieving parents, horrific as it is.

Besides those feelings of hopelessness, when I first entered the land of the grieving, I also felt like Dorothy in Oz. There were vaguely familiar reminders of a world I once knew, but in my tragically altered existence, everything was askew, murky. In contrast to Dorothy, however, there was no obvious yellow brick road for me to follow through the strange new territory. Along with my own "munchkins," I had landed in surroundings that were not only unfamiliar and bizarre, but dismal and scary.

To complicate things further, grief siphoned my reserves of faith and hope, which had always been my personal motivators. I was one of the lucky parents, though; life had provided me with other motivators, namely Davin, Lauren, and Greg. Thankfully, love for my three surviving children propelled me into each day, and together we carried on. Beyond that, we were reinforced from every angle by a blending of people who never gave up on our healthy recovery.

Generations of relatives, a multitude of friends, and even strangers made my children and me the objects of their loving support when Neil engaged the fight for his life. Every one of them remains immortalized in our hearts, but for fear of overlooking even one such person, I have refrained from listing them en masse. Instead, I have decided to introduce you to one person who had an unexpected role in my family's emotional and spiritual recovery: Judy was the friend who delivered me to my first heartifact. The game-changing event initiated a journey of healing that no one could have anticipated.

Like so many others, Judy made notable contributions of time and energy toward my family's well-being during Neil's struggle with cancer. But that fact did not replace her usual concerns for her own family. During the same time period, Judy's aging mother needed her support back home in Southern California, where Judy also had grown children. It was logical for her to return to her roots, but the thought of such a dear friend moving so far away saddened me. Understandably, Judy's mother needed her daughter as much as Neil needed me.

Several months of real-estate marketing finally led to the sale of Judy's Pittsburgh home. This was good news on one hand, and disturbing news on the other—the timing was tragic. Judy ended up departing Pittsburgh permanently within days of Neil's funeral. Suddenly, thousands of miles separated me from one of my stalwarts. We both felt the distance, but Judy was not dissuaded from keeping me under her protective radar. Within weeks, I received an invitation to be her first house guest in the seaside village of Carlsbad.

At first I hesitated to leave my three surviving children so soon after losing Neil. Upon further consideration, I concluded that a brief change of scenery might help me recover more rapidly from all that had happened. What Judy offered to me (besides her loyal friendship) were megadoses of restorative sunshine and salt air. Finally, I accepted her invitation. I hoped the trip would jump-start an emotional and spiritual revival for me. After determining that my children would be in good hands during my absence, I gratefully accepted Judy's invitation. A short time later, I was airborne and headed westward.

I landed at San Diego International Airport about five hours later. Judy met me at baggage claim. It was so nice to be in my dear friend's company again, but I noticed her greeting was a careful one. (I sensed that Judy, as a mother herself, could hardly grasp that I was living without one of my children.) She then led me to her car, and as we walked, I took in all of San Diego's inviting scenery. I delighted in the sway of the palm trees, the intensity of the blue skies, the vibrancy of the local foliage, and the gentleness of the breeze from the seaside harbor. For a moment, I felt relieved of the difficulties I had endured in Pittsburgh. My new environs were delicious by comparison, and I was grateful for that.

Once we reached Judy's vehicle, we loaded ourselves and our belongings into it. Then she inquired, "So, Maggie, what is the first thing you'd like to do now that you are here?"

Without much forethought or hesitation, I replied, "Let's head to the beach and catch the sunset." It was an idea that came out of nowhere.

I privately pondered my own suggestion. Then I took it a step further; I imagined how sweet being "christened" in the same ocean Neil had enjoyed a year earlier would be. During the summer of 2000, Neil had joined some of his West Coast relatives to celebrate the conclusion of his cancer treatments. Part of his fun included boating and bodysurfing in the Pacific Ocean. His Cali trip was his proverbial victory lap. It also marked the beginning of one of the happiest periods of his life.

Without being privy to all of my musings, Judy replied, "No problem! Let's find a sunset for you, Maggie."

Judy then pulled her car away from the curb at the airport terminal, and we headed north on Interstate 5. About a half hour later we arrived at Carlsbad Beach, and there it was…the most incredible sunset I have ever seen! The spent day was melting like gold into the cool horizon far across the expansive body of water before me. Then it struck me: tomorrow would soon be on its way, along with an endless sea of possibilities.

As we both emerged from the car, I exclaimed to Judy, "This sunset is more breathtaking than I could have ever imagined!"

But seeing it from where we were standing was not enough for me. I wanted more. For this reason, I asked Judy to open the trunk of her car. She didn't mind, but I could tell she wondered why.

"I need to get my swimsuit," I offered, as she popped the trunk open remotely.

My friend obliged, but she also expressed her doubts that my idea was a good one.

"Are you planning to go into the water, Maggie?" Judy inquired with disbelief.

"I am," I stated.

"Well, I can tell you've never been in the Pacific Ocean in April before!" she retorted, tongue in cheek. "It is going to be freezing, Maggie, especially this late in the day."

"I will be okay, Judy. I promise," I answered nonchalantly.

A truer answer would have been, "I'm not sure I have a choice, Judy!" For some reason, I had to get closer to that sunset. Not Judy, though; she had a choice, and hers was to stay warm and dry.

"Maggie, no one is in the water tonight...not even the surfers! And if they were, I assure you, they'd be wearing wetsuits!"

Undeterred, I waved her off, smiled, and entered the surf alone.

Judy was right about the water, after all; it was *frigid*! By the time I was up to my shoulders in it, I was numb and shivering uncontrollably. Thankfully, the vivid spectacle of the sunset, ablaze with unearthly colors, mesmerized me and distracted me from my chilly discomfort. The palette on the horizon was gold, orange, and red, woven through with shades of indigo. Its intensity continued to draw me closer.

As I faced the lit sky in my semi-frozen condition, I considered whether I should duck my head under the ice-cold water (and totally acclimate to its temperature) or simply retreat back to the shore. But before I had time to make a choice, I was consumed with pain— emotional, spiritual, pit-of-my-gut pain—a beast I had held at bay up until that moment. The grief housed in every recess of my being was about to erupt, and I was powerless to stop it. Then came the tears; they rushed forth in torrents as my chest heaved and convulsed with the force of my sobs. Without warning, my grief announced itself. It would no longer be contained. Three years' worth of loss and sadness became the force behind the wall that was about to burst. The virtual dam that was once my heart finally gave way. I felt it shatter.

As I sobbed toward that beautiful, compassionate sunset, I released a mother lode of grief to all of creation. I had lost so much: my marriage, my mother, but most of all, Neil.

And it hurt.

Everything hurt.

I was as alone as I could be in the wake of a life gone sideways. I wasn't just sad anymore, either; I was angry.

In searching desperation, my thoughts shifted to the only conceivable source of all this misery: my Creator...my God. Feeling completely broken, my thoughts, rooted in despair, suddenly surged up from a place beneath my sadness. Unleashed, my mind boldly petitioned God:

"What in the world happened to my family, Lord? What else could you possibly want from me?"

From my perspective, I had nothing to lose by asking. I already felt abandoned. I also felt that heaven owed me an explanation for the one-two-three punch of life-altering losses.

"How on earth do I face another day?" I pleaded to God, with His universe as my witness.

Then, wracked with that unfamiliar depth of grief and exhaustion, an even darker thought intruded and took advantage of my vulnerability: a compassionate God would free me of all this pain, wouldn't He? Perhaps He could just sweep me out to sea this very night.

In my mind, I was just "done."

But just as suddenly as my spiritual tantrum had emerged, my sensibilities returned. The brazen, self-indulgent phantom that had joined me in the ocean that night was now a foreigner to me. Giving up had never been my style. I knew I had much to live for; I just didn't know where to start.

"God," I pleaded, "what am I to do with grief that stares back at me everywhere I turn? I know I cannot retrieve all that I have lost, but at the very least, can you provide me with some direction? I cannot take much more."

Then, as if an alarm sounded, my thoughts were interrupted and my attention shifted. I was suddenly aware that my decision to take a sunset swim in the Pacific Ocean was not only dicey, but dangerous! I was tempting fate in the tumultuous night surf, and it was gaining momentum as the seconds passed. Sand and ocean debris began swirling around my legs as my mind conjured up a new thought altogether: what about sharks? I was sure I had heard of Southern California swimmers and surfers falling victim to the notorious sea predators at one time or another.

Self-preservation suddenly became my primary focus, so I glanced toward the beach, my refuge. My intuition must have been spot-on; Judy was waving me in frantically when I caught sight of her.

A feeling of panic then washed over me as the most obvious fact of all flashed across my mind like a neon billboard: "Your three surviving children are also struggling with the loss of Neil, Maggie. You are their mother too. You need to pull yourself together."

"I had better get out of here!" I declared to myself.

The time had come for me to retreat to dry land. Meanwhile, indistinct underwater objects began relentlessly thrashing my legs. I wasn't sure if I was being struck by seashells, driftwood, stones, or possibly even marine life; so many unidentifiable things were bouncing off of my lower extremities. Throughout this commotion one particular item caught my attention as it knocked at me repeatedly, just above my ankles. The strikes did not hurt me, but they felt somewhat deliberate. This was strange, especially since the power of the tide was amplifying simultaneously. Finally, the dramatic scene ignited a grief-fueled fearlessness within me, and I ducked underwater to intercept the persistent object.

Ahh! I thought, as my tear-swollen face felt some relief. The glacial temperature of the ocean water soothed my overworked tear ducts and puffy eyes.

Beneath its surface, I searched for whatever had been rapping at my legs in the water, but I could see nothing in the dank, chaotic abyss. Instead, I grabbed for whatever I might grasp in the vicinity of my ankles, and then resurfaced. I came up with something, but what?

In order to find out, I instinctively squeezed the burning salt water from my eyes. Then I loosened my grip on the object and took a peek. I was stunned at what I saw. I had retrieved a perfectly heart-shaped stone!

Image 3. Neil's heart box with first heartifact (Carlsbad, CA, April 2001)

"*No way!*" I said, as I looked toward the sky.

Then an unusual calm came over me. I suddenly felt peaceful and safe.

I immediately wondered if the heart stone in my hand was God's reply to my desperate pleadings. This possibility humbled me, for I had petitioned Him only moments before. I was also perplexed at the distinct closeness I suddenly felt to my deceased son. The newfound token of hope struck awe in me.

"How in the world could a stone leave me feeling so close to my God and my son?" I pondered.

"One incontrovertible heart," I whispered to myself.

It seemed my sweet heart-giver, Neil, was at it again. And I felt so lucky as a result. Discovering the distinctive stone made everything just a little more "right." It even justified my questionable choice to enter the foreboding ocean in the first place. Apparently, that was *exactly* what I needed to do that night.

Feeling protected and deeply contented by now, I was ready to heed Judy's hand signals from the shore and return to where I had left her. In fact, I could not wait! Swimming ashore proved to be a bigger challenge than entering the surf had been, however. The tide had become more aggressive since then, and now I was one of the objects being tossed about in the sea. Ocean debris continued to pound against my body while each new wave swelled up and then spit me out like a gigantic exhale from Poseidon, the mythological god of the sea. On a couple occasions I was able to huddle beneath the night tide for a momentary reprieve and savor the stillness—the silence. That was also when I blindly gathered up a couple more undersea items and added them to the first. I held on to all of them tightly but did not dare take time to examine the second and third objects; the waves were too daunting.

Inch by inch, each new wave lobbed me toward Judy until I eventually made it to shallower water. Finally, I was able to get some footing in the drenched sands of the shoreline and pull myself upright again. Trudging out of the raucous tide, I then purposefully headed toward my anxious friend with my full hands clasped against my chest.

By the time I reached her I was shivering and completely disheveled, but happy, too. I could not wait to reveal my ocean bounty to my landlubber friend. And crazily enough, as I did this, I saw not one but *three* heart-shaped stones! I could not believe it! Each one was about the same size, but otherwise the stones were unique. Judy shared my curiosity about what was in my hands, but not to the same extent. The three Pacific Ocean heart stones represented far more than beach souvenirs to me. I regarded them as blessings…maybe even miracles!

Image 4. Heartifacts one, two & three (Carlsbad, CA, April 2001)

I then asked Judy, "Are heart-shaped rocks something for which Carlsbad Beach is known?"

Cheekily, she replied, "Gnarly waves and hard-bodied surfers are this beach's only trademarks, Maggie!"

Judy continued, "I have never found a heart-shaped stone…not here or anywhere else. I think these are very unique, Maggie."

I was beginning to discern a purpose behind what had unfolded since my arrival in San Diego, but I was not ready to reveal my private thoughts to anyone. My "moment" with God was also too personal to divulge. Instead, Judy was free to draw her own conclusions about the heart rocks. She examined them thoroughly and then smiled. By then, I believe her intuitive powers were kicking in.

"Interesting," was all she said.

In slightly maternal fashion, Judy then expressed her relief that I had gotten out of the harrowing night surf unscathed. I was relieved, too, but in retrospect I was more interested in why I felt so drawn to the situation in the first place. Something much stronger than good sense had called me into the ocean that night. Something had beckoned me. Perhaps I had been guided into the isolation of the ocean at dusk so I could be free to release my fears and find healing. Perhaps the sunset was heaven's bait. (God knows, my broken heart and spirit were in need of some serious repair by then.) But I know one thing for sure: the heart-shaped symbols of love that made their way from the ocean floor to me initiated my recovery from years of loss.

Yes, my compounded grief met its match in the ocean at Carlsbad, and I had an inexplicable sense that my deceased son, Neil, was heavily involved. Surely, the heart stones that found me that night were not random. They were meant precisely for me and provided to me when I needed them most…gifts from the indomitable spirit of my son.

Neil had given hearts to me throughout his lifetime, and that is why "heartifacts" matter to me. The first one alone made my grief manageable. The ones that have surfaced since reinforce my healing and enable me to help other families who grieve for sons and daughters. In a sense, my first heartifact broke my grief apart and swept it out to sea. But more than that, heartifacts remind me that I continue to be surrounded by my son's love even though his mortal life is over. I thank God for making such a miracle possible, and I thank Him for His endless mercy and grace.

The remainder of my week in California could not have been better, but by the time it came to an end, I was ready to return to Pittsburgh. I had so much to share with my kids! My carry-on bag contained three unique treasures from the sea, and my heart was filled with encouragement. Perhaps heaven and Neil were not so far away! I flew home bearing hearts that only heaven and earth could have created. I could hardly wait for my plane to land!

When I arrived home, it did not take long for me to share the dramatic story of my first evening in California. Davin, seventeen, Lauren, thirteen, and Greg, nine, embraced the significance of the heart stones without question; Neil always did have a certain magic about him. Besides that, the kids could tell *Mom was back*...really back.

On that day, my kids and I claimed the Carlsbad heart stones as our quiet little miracles and placed them atop our mantel. To us, the new heartifacts represented Neil's continued spiritual presence in our lives. In other words, Neil was back, too! But something my kids and I never imagined was that the three heart stones from California were just the beginning of an ever-growing collection. As I will now demonstrate, unusual hearts continue to "rock" our world.

FIVE

AFFIRMATIONS

After Neil's passing in March of 2001, Davin, Lauren, and Greg still had the rest of their school year to complete. And by June, they had really earned some fun and relaxation. My sister, Pat, and brother-in-law, Paul, who resided near Houston, Texas, sensed this and suggested a plan. They thought a visit to the YO Ranch, located in their state's Hill Country, would be a perfect place for such adventure to unfold. I agreed; their plan represented a brand-new positive experience, a complete distraction from what my children had endured during the previous couple of years in Pittsburgh. It also gave them an opportunity to retrace some of Neil's happiest steps; he and I had enjoyed the same Texas excursion a year earlier, shortly after his trip to California. At the time, Neil was on top of the world. Before his siblings and I knew it, Paul and Pat finalized arrangements for our visit.

The kids and I were lavished with healing doses of Southern hospitality from the moment we landed at George Bush Intercontinental

Airport. After collecting our suitcases from baggage claim, we were greeted by a limousine driver who was holding a sign that read, "Maggie and Kids." I smiled when I saw that. Leon, the driver Paul had sent, then introduced himself to us.

"Let the distracting commence!" I uttered to myself.

My trio and I felt like celebrities as Leon sped us toward Paul and Pat's house in Katy, Texas. Once there, we unwound in their swimming pool and then went over our itinerary for the week ahead with our host and hostess. Paul was a planner, and did he ever love Texas! By early the next morning, we were loaded into their Chevy Suburban and off to Paul and Pat's cabin at the YO Ranch.

As you can probably tell, my sister and her husband, the Wolkenbergs, were components of the human circle of support that had formed around my children and me since 1998. As their thoughtfulness and generosity manifested, I was moved to count the blessings that were showering my little family of survivors. We had so much to appreciate, despite what life had dished out.

As hundreds of miles fell behind us on our way across Texas, I was astounded by the blankets of blue that bordered the highways we traveled. They had been created by an abundance of the state flower, the Texas blue bonnet. The bountiful fields of the distinctive blossoms seemed to mirror the azure sky above us. The blue surrounding us that day was as vibrant as the colors of the first sunset I had seen in Carlsbad. And the timing of this new display seemed perfect. You see, during our Texas road trip, another thing had become apparent; the children and I were not grieving in isolation. *Everyone* in the family missed two very important people: Grandma Ev and Neil, Pat's godson. Our being wrapped in the tranquil scene felt like a prolonged and powerful hug from heaven and earth. The embrace nature provided that day was something all of us needed. It was a big hug, too— like Paul's plans for our week. A Texan would have it no other way!

Image 5. Greg, Maggie, Lauren & Davin (Texas Hill Country, June 2001)

Despite all of our emotional attachments, Paul made it his job to keep the spirit of the week light. He had packed so much into our sightseeing agenda; we had no choice but to keep moving. Wisdom must have told him that constant motion would be the best way to keep each of us from ruminating over sad thoughts for too long. Without being insensitive, Paul did his best to steer us away from the feelings grief usually engendered.

One of the favorite distractions Paul had arranged for us was a tubing adventure down the Guadalupe River. During this gentle river ride, the children and I were surprised with more heart stones…five of them! We were not intentionally cultivating one, but suddenly we had a bona fide collection of the unusual rocks.

Image 6. First eight heartifacts (California & Texas, spring 2001)

When we showed our Texas heart stones to Paul and Pat, they found them to be unique and interesting, but not necessarily laden with the significance we had attached to them; then again, I had not yet told them about my Carlsbad experience. To my children and me, however, the additional heart stones were profound! We had not been looking for them as we floated down the Guadalupe. They just happened to be in our path! We decided: Pat and Paul needed to know the *whole* story in order to appreciate our enthusiasm.

My sister and her husband enjoyed our tale, but they absorbed it cautiously. I could tell they did not want to feed into anything that might be construed as an unhealthy adaptation to grief. Both of them wanted only the best for us, including complete emotional well-being. We had lost a lot.

But among ourselves, the kids and I giggled, "What do they know about hearts?"

Having five new (and unexpected) heart stones in our possession was nothing but reassuring to us. Encouraged, we secretly vowed to remain in the positive flow our new blessings had created. We felt certain that whatever was blossoming before our eyes was something extraordinary.

By the end of our Texas visit, we were calling our heart-shaped stones heartifacts, a made-up word meaning "artifacts of love." For us, they represented Neil's love, and the amazing little miracles added momentum to our journey of healing from the hurt of losing him. We knew that we were being provided with something of great significance...significance we had yet to fully understand.

SIX

THE CAPE OF HEARTS

Judging from the trips I have described, one thing is very clear: my children and I were showered with the compassion of many caring people during and after Neil's ordeal. Toward the end of the summer in 2001, we were recipients of yet one more of those extra special opportunities.

A graduate of my high school reached out in a very generous way after learning about all that my children and I had been through between 1998 and 2001. Her brother, Ed, was a classmate and friend of mine. Helen, his sister, owned a fully equipped vacation home in Cape May, New Jersey, and she wanted to make it available to my children and me. Through Ed, she offered us a weeklong stay in the seaside town. I was humbled by Helen's thoughtfulness, especially since I barely knew her. I accepted her invitation with gratitude I could not begin to fully express. Knowing how restorative my April visit to the Pacific Ocean had been for me, I felt certain that time at the Atlantic would be at least as healing for my children.

On our way to Cape May from Pittsburgh, the road trip had been basically uneventful, and I was very happy for this. As the only adult among us during the seven-hour trip, driving had been my sole responsibility. After crossing northern Maryland, however, I enjoyed being relieved of those duties for a bit. That is when we drove aboard the Lewes Ferry, which carried us across the Delaware Bay. This mode of transportation represented a totally new experience for my children. At first, being on the huge barge was exciting, but the novelty slowly wore off. During our voyage, each one of us seemed to drift into our own thoughts of nostalgia. We were remembering other beach vacations, and grief was creeping in again.

Two distinct realities loomed large that day: the children and I were still getting used to the new configuration of our family, and visiting the Atlantic Ocean was something we had never done without Neil or their dad. Not only that, my in-laws had lived near the same shore during their retirement, and visiting them had been our annual family vacation for over ten years. It was strange to be headed in that direction with so many persons missing.

The ferry floated directly to the shore of the quaint little village. As the huge vessel docked in Cape May, we got back into our car. Thankfully, our enthusiasm for the vacation at hand returned the closer we got to the salty sea. As each car funneled toward the boat's narrow exit, the process of disembarking reminded me of schoolchildren lining up to be released for recess. By now, we just wanted to be on our way.

Once back on dry pavement, and just as we had detected progress toward our final destination, we were delayed again. The first traffic signal we encountered in Cape May turned from amber to red as we approached it.

"Ugh!" my edgy passengers and I sighed in unison.

We could hardly stand another interruption on our way to the beach. When we finally came to a complete stop in the line of traffic, something on the car directly in front of us shifted my mood immediately. This particular vehicle sported a license plate that seemed to be put there just for us.

I gasped, "Hey, kids, look at that license!"

I pointed through our car's windshield. In order to see where I was directing their attention, the three kids promptly scrambled from their slouched positions. Davin, Lauren, and Greg then joined in my delight at what was etched across the Maryland plate: *N-E-I-L*.

Seeing this lifted our spirits instantly. Inspired by this reminder of Neil, we became energized and wondered what other good things would manifest during our Cape May visit.

As the week unfolded, we were far from disappointed. To describe our week in Cape May as magical would be an understatement—"enchanting" was closer to the truth. Our 2001 beach vacation in New Jersey turned out to be just perfect; even the weather cooperated.

Every day was a beach day, and we hauled our beach essentials to the shore each morning like it was our job! Regardless of where I positioned my chair and beach umbrella, once I settled into my post (for keeping an eye on my swimmers), a heart stone was within reach! I know it sounds unbelievable, but heart stones and seashells seemed to be everywhere we looked, all week long. It was ludicrous! We were even swimming among them!

I exclaimed to my children, "No one will *ever* believe this heart thing!"

The special week in Cape May also included my first birthday since Neil's passing. I expected that it would be a tender one, but our being bombarded with more and more hearts from the sea made up for this. I was excited and amazed by what was happening. With the exception of Pat and Paul in Texas, however, I was still sensitive about discussing our heartifacts with anyone other than my kids. Outsiders might think I was sliding down a slippery emotional slope and dragging my children along with me.

We would see.

Also anticipating that my birthday might be a difficult day for me, my father, another of my sisters, and one of her sons joined us for a couple of days. We felt very fortunate to have Pop Pop, Joyce, and Sean in the mix. I think our high spirits surprised them at first; but in no time, at least Joyce and Sean realized why my kids and I were feeling so lighthearted (no pun intended). My dad, on the other hand, remained very introspective. He was struggling through grief for Neil and my mother in his own way…the usual way.

Although I know he wanted my birthday to be a happy one, my father still missed my mother terribly when he arrived in Cape May. Of course he did; the first anniversary of her August 15 death was approaching. Compounding that, he ached over the additional cancer death of his teenage grandson. His outliving Neil and Evelyn were hideous and incomprehensible for Pop Pop; thus, heart-shaped rocks and shells held no significance to him. In fact, they were practically an insult, in his opinion. I completely understood his point of view, but could not discount the ongoing madcap phenomenon. It was truly outrageous! My children and I did not ask for heartifacts, nor seek them; we simply ran with them. Our being intoxicated with hearts felt so much better than being inconsolably sad. Besides, Neil would have despised the latter.

The hearts nature produced for us did not relent all week long. In fact, they showed up with more bizarre regularity as the days passed. I specifically noticed this when Joyce joined me for daily walks along the strand. Our strolls yielded so many heartifacts that the pockets of our shorts bulged with them.

By the time my children and I left Cape May, we felt like seafarers who had recovered a lost treasure: Neil. Our New Jersey heartifacts reiterated that his loving and playful spirit was everywhere! Why wouldn't we feel richer for that? Returning to Pittsburgh with a bucket full of new heartifacts was something we never anticipated, but we loved adding them to the eight that were waiting at home.

Image 7. Heartifacts heart, our growing collection (August 2001)

SEVEN

FULL-GROWN HEARTIFACT

As if to punctuate the first full year of discovering heart rocks, I literally tromped upon one of my absolute favorites on June 30, 2002. The date was meaningful, for it would have been Neil's twenty-first birthday. Noticing a heartifact on what might have been an overwhelmingly emotional day validated the mystical, comforting, and healing nature of those symbolic stones all over again. On this momentous day, Davin, Lauren, Greg, and I decided to picnic in the Laurel Mountains near Neil's favorite local destination, Seven Springs Ski Resort.

Neil had been an avid skier. Since his first ski trip with a busload of junior high classmates, he was hooked on the winter sport. He loved the freedom and exhilaration of downhill skiing, and some of his happiest times were spent "hitting" moguls. Along with his friends, he loved to challenge himself by conquering the advanced "black diamond" slopes on the snow-covered mountains of Champion, Pennsylvania. Skiing eventually edged out many of Neil's usual favorite pastimes—well, except for eating.

Though it is hard for me to admit, I believe food was Neil's first love. And over time, he became a creative and enthusiastic connoisseur. At least that is what his family and friends will confirm. We all knew a meal was far more than a requirement of living for Neil; it was an event! It is true—my first son was a dining enthusiast long before he ever clicked into a ski binding.

Even his voicemail greeting confirmed as much by saying, "Hi. This is Neil, and if I didn't answer my cell phone, I am probably eating."

My point about Neil's love of food, you ask? Well, if we could have snow skied to commemorate his twenty-first birthday, we surely would have. Unfortunately, there is no snow skiing in Pennsylvania on June 30. Forced to go another route, we chose food. A special picnic near Neil's most loved mountains proved to be perfect.

Many members of our extended family were able to join us that day. Consequently, my kids and I prepared a mobile feast as though we were entering a county fair cook-off. When we reached our destination, we were delighted that our favorite picnic grove (next to our favorite mountain stream) was available. A lush forest of pines and mountain laurels created a perfect canopy under which we celebrated the landmark anniversary of Neil's birth and happy life.

Once we found this ideal location devoid of other picnickers, each car in our family caravan pulled off the narrow mountain road and promptly parked. Our car doors flew open, and we spilled from our seats like twelfth graders on the last day of high school. Everyone hurried toward the narrow bridge that crossed the bubbling creek— that is, everyone except for me.

I was left behind with a food-laden cooler, looking for the shortest distance to the prized picnic spot. Flashing back to my childhood creek-hopping days, I decided to conserve my steps and go directly through the chilly stream instead of traversing the bridge.

I recall thinking, "I'll get wet, but it's a picnic, not a formal."

My route also proved to be the most rewarding one.

The swiftly moving, ever-changing stream required that I choose my stepping stones carefully; otherwise, the cooler and I were sure to take a plunge. Proceeding cautiously, I made it to the last of the creek stones that had paved a path for me through the water. While standing upon it, I looked down and my jaw dropped in disbelief. Beneath my feet was an enormous, distinctly heart-shaped rock!

Image 8. Neil's twenty-first birthday heartifact, beneath the original (June 30, 2002)

Without budging another inch, I planted both of my feet on the newest heartifact and called for my nearest son, Greg. The ten-year-old raced over to me and confirmed my impression.

"You're standing on a *huge* heart rock, Mom!" he exclaimed.

Then, in his excitement, he nearly pulled the jumbo-sized stone out from under me! For my own good, I continued to the bank of the creek to relieve myself of the cooler. Then I looked back at Greg—only to see him holding the gigantic rock up against his chest! I was stunned that he had lifted it off the creek bed by himself! Neither the weight of the rock, icy water, slimy mud, nor pinchers of crayfish (hidden beneath such rocks) had stopped him.

When we made eye contact, Greg proclaimed, "This one is ours!"

My youngest had been dubbed "Bubba" during the very first days of his life, and the brawny feat I just described demonstrates why the nickname applied to him. Hugging the huge rock, with mud dripping through his hands and down his belly, Greg lugged the find back across the stream and up an embankment to dump it into the trunk of my car.

For his own reasons, Greg never doubted that our family maintained a supernatural connection with Neil. That is why Greg embraced the heart stone legacy without question from the very start. When his eldest brother's twenty-first birthday heartifact appeared, it just reinforced what Greg already knew about Neil's dedication to his family in a distinctive and demonstrative way. Today it is still the grandest of our heart rocks.

To this day, my family and friends delight in finding heart stones at the most random times and in the most random places. There is no need to search for them; honestly, they just show up! And when they do, the news still travels fast.

Image 9. Grown-up Greg with another heartifact (2010)

Finding heartifacts is *absolutely* the softer side of our journey since losing Neil to cancer. Obviously, no person or thing (even the most meaningful reminder of a loved one) can replace that person. My children and I accept the hearts manifesting in our lives as tangible tokens of hope. That is all. For us, they are symbolic treasures representing the love of a devoted son and brother. *They are not idols.* We welcome the spirit of the hearts. It validates our faith in eternal love, and that is far better than giving death the power to sever Neil from us for the rest of our earthly lives. Death is of the body. Love is of the Spirit. Heartifacts represent love.

EIGHT

SOLIDARITY

There is a little more you should know about my initial speaking engagement at the Children's Hospital of Pittsburgh. When I declared that an unexpected and insistent heart-shaped stone had transformed my own grief into hope, I assure you, no one expected it. Sometimes I still cannot believe I ever gave a speech about rocks during a memorial service for the children of complete strangers. I admit, I was leading my audience into murky waters, and it was a risky tack to take. My departure from a straight and narrow path through grief required that I surrender to faith and allow myself to follow guidance from the spirit of my deceased son. Remember, it was input from Neil that compelled the writing of my first speech. Once that happened, I did not question the plan. I just followed through.

For the sake of other families wrestling with grief for a child, I was inspired to expose my family's secret weapon against the dark foe. How my family survived Neil's death with any grace at all had everything to do with the surprising signs that sprung forth out of my deepest grief for him. This was the best news I could share with families in such horrendous pain. When I first agreed to assist the Memorial Service Planning Committee, I had no idea I would end up sharing such a personal story. At that time, I was sure of one thing only: I wanted to help. In the end, revealing my family's heartifact phenomenon was definitely the right course to take. I know this now because it worked! *Truth always works.* And my testimony was nothing more than a truthful account of what had really happened to me. Every time I reveal a heart stone, truth speaks for itself.

Thankfully, I was not invited to *prove* anything or make sense of grief. I was included as one who knew it firsthand. I was still processing it, surviving it, with an audience who was trying to do the same. In total, we had witnessed the lives and deaths of dozens of beloved children. Nothing about that made sense. What did seem logical to me was to offer my audience something I had (apparently) been groomed to provide to them. When the story of my original heartifact landed softly on the hearts of all who had gathered for the memorial, I felt I was right where I belonged. I will explain.

While waiting to deliver that first speech, I sat among nearly two hundred bereaved family members. I was surrounded by grieving, wall-to-wall grieving. The sadness in the room was nearly suffocating. Suddenly, I felt extra nervous and torn about what I intended to talk about; the magnitude of addressing such loss was intimidating. My grief, the bear that sometimes roared and sometimes hibernated, was now cavorting in a den packed with the grief of a couple hundred others! How dare I reveal my unconventional heart-stone story to such an unpredictable group? But it was too late for me to change course. Therefore, I stuck to my plan and delivered the most hopeful and sincere message I could offer. I knew that my heartifacts and I would either hit the mark or fail miserably. I was left to simply trust.

Fortunately, I did not estrange anyone with what I shared that day. In fact, the opposite occurred; applause broke out when I concluded my portion of the program. Yes, applause! It was something that seemed almost inappropriate during such a solemn gathering. I was relieved that the story had made a positive impact. The group, which had previously shown significant signs of distress, seemed to come alive with the hope provided by the story I shared. There was obvious curiosity and enthusiasm about the legend of heartifacts!

Reverend Freeman and his fellow committee members were pleased, too. The crowd's unsolicited positive reaction validated the trust they had placed in me. Their demonstrative approval of the story, and the gratitude extended to me for sharing it, was powerful. My decision to trust my instincts and inspiration was affirmed. Clearly, I had been guided well.

I thanked God that the speech had gone well. I also thanked Him for keeping Neil alive in my heart. I needed him there.

When the clapping subsided and the room became silent again, I found myself locked in a puzzling stare with my audience. In my mind, I had already said all I had planned to say. A few more awkward moments passed as I processed the scene. My mind searched for what to do next.

Then I surmised (to myself), "This group wants something more from me—but what?"

Next, my mind switched from searching to racing. At a loss, I turned to Reverend Freeman, hoping for a reprieve, but he just grinned calmly in return.

He and I both knew something good had just happened in that room. My story had stirred something huge…something healing… something spiritual.

Still, I was the one on the stage in the proverbial hot seat—alone!

From my vantage point I could see that the faces before me, somber and tear-streaked at the start of my speech, had changed for the better after hearing it. The angst of the audience had dissipated, and there was a new mood in the room; innocence, wonder, and hope replaced heartache and distress. The moment reminded me of how I felt when I discovered my first heartifact. Again, I was astounded.

"Oh my goodness," I thought in silence. "It's the magic of the heart stones...This crowd totally gets it!"

Then, as if someone had snapped me out of a trance, I knew exactly what my audience members wanted. They were waiting to see my original heart stone for themselves.

"How could I have *not* planned for that?" I bashfully wondered.

"How did I leave out the most pertinent thing of all?" I murmured to myself.

It was now my turn to "get it." If just hearing my story could calm a grief-saturated room, maybe seeing and touching an authentic heartifact would magnify the effect of the message.

Thankfully, I had grabbed my first heartifact and dropped it into my blazer pocket as I bolted from my house that morning. Although bringing it along had been a complete afterthought, I had clutched the stone like a baby clutches a blanket throughout my entire presentation! Perhaps my subconscious had nudged me to take it along at the last minute, or perhaps I had been compelled to do so by another source altogether. All I know is this: I was glad I had my Carlsbad heart stone close at hand when all those wanting eyes were locked on me at the conclusion of my first speech.

As I raised my hand and revealed my hidden heart stone, calmness washed over the room. Hushed murmurs of *ooh* and *aah* spread across the auditorium. Everyone present, including me, instantly knew their own hearts, their wounded hearts, were in a safe and secure forum. From my perspective, a new kinship had been forged among us, and we all understood one thing: *we were bound together by the love each of us held for a child we'd had to let go.* The simple act of offering my own broken heart from behind that podium, along with the one that held it together, was enough to shine a ray of hope into the bleak auditorium. I was so grateful for the warm and careful reaction to the heartifact I displayed that I was moved to release it to the audience.

Prior to that morning, my inaugural heart stone had never left my house. It held a special place on the mantel of my hearth, secure in my home. But following the first speech I gave at a memorial service, sharing my most treasured heartifact with my new comrades in grief suddenly seemed like the perfect thing to do. In fact, it felt like the necessary thing to do.

I processed all of these thoughts in a fraction of a second (although it felt like forever to me). Then I asked the people before me, "Would you like to *see* the heart stone?"

My question was answered by a sea of nodding heads that seemed to say, "Do you really need to ask?"

In response, I handed my first California heart stone to Pastor Freeman. He followed my cue and then passed it to the nearest parent. This continued until the stone made its way through the entire audience. I was truly mesmerized as each bereaved person held it, examined it, pondered it, and then passed it on to the next. I witnessed the birth of a tradition—a healing and bonding tradition.

Since the first spontaneous relaying of Neil's heart stone in April 2005, I have asked those who touch it to infuse it with the love they feel for their own deceased child. I also invite them to receive the same encouragement and healing I felt when I first found it. It is a reminder that heaven has limitless ways to reach each of us.

To me, the uncontrived tradition also represents solidarity among families who have suffered the loss of a child. Very few words are needed between such people. When grieving parents and siblings reveal themselves to one another, bridges can be built, memories can be shared, and lives can be honored without apology. No one should have to face the loss of a child alone. It is just too hard.

Passing the stone was certainly the best way to close the story I had just shared. Beyond that, I learned that doing so resulted in something even more profound: *experiencing* the heartifact, firsthand, allowed each grieving person who touched it permission to consider the illogical and improbable ways of the universe. Sharing what God had given to me seemed to give the other grieving families permission to believe that a connection with their child, though deceased, is possible. Every grieving parent I have met hopes for such communication. Thus my good news was their good news.

Perhaps all children who have passed on can find a supernatural way to reach their loving earth families. Heartifacts force me to assume this much is possible. Neil's spirit absolutely continues to impact my family's life in many positive ways. Therefore, I suggest that any loving family who grieves for a child can consider themselves an expanded family instead of a depleted one. This type of acceptance will not happen overnight, however; it takes time, an open mind, and a heart that is softened. My experience has taught me many things, but two in particular: that love transcends all limitations, including time, space, and mortality; and that a family bound by love never dies—it lives on in the heart of each loving member.

NINE

DREAM OR REALITY CHECK?

Like other parents, I have dreamt about all of my children at one time or another, but dreaming about a deceased child is far different. For me, it has been a bittersweet experience. While I long for any chance to catch a glimpse of Neil, awakening from dream events of this nature usually leave me feeling empty and sad, as though my precious son has been snatched away from me all over again. It is difficult to awaken to the realization that he is still gone. For better or worse, I have had relatively few dreams of Neil since he died, but one does stand out—especially considering the notion of solidarity I presented in the last chapter.

In this particular Neil dream, I was standing before a landscape of gently rolling hills covered with lush green grass. It was the kind of landscape I imagine I will see in Ireland someday. On the horizon, far off to the right, the emerald land met an intensely blue sky. As I continued looking in that direction, I saw a white line forming on the crest of the farthest hill. The longer I looked at it, the thicker the white line became. It seemed to be pulsing toward me like an iridescent wave.

Gently and steadily, the bright band grew thicker as it got closer to me. Finally, I could see that thousands of children in simple white garments created the illusion. They were a happy bunch, but surprisingly calm, too. As the playful group continued to flow from my right to my left, I was mesmerized by the breathtaking procession. With no particular urgency, it proceeded past me toward a destination somewhere off to my left and out of my sight.

Next, I panned back to the right and became even more drawn in by the scene. I noticed something new. Someone twice as tall as all of the children was now coming from the original horizon. My eyes remained fixed on the figure as it moved closer. Very smoothly and decisively, the taller figure stopped in front of me and then turned to face me. That was also when my eyes focused more precisely, and I recognized the full-grown figure.

It was Neil.

I was ecstatic to see my departed son standing before me so handsome and whole—all six feet of him! I was also delighted that there was no evidence of the cancer that had left Neil wheelchair-bound before he died. All I wanted to do at that point was approach him and steal a hug. I knew dream time was fickle and that Neil's image could vanish as quickly as it had appeared. A flurry of questions stormed my mind; besides embracing my child, there was so much I wanted to ask him. But for some reason that I cannot explain, I knew I could not get any closer to Neil. Consequently, I did not budge an inch or say a word in my dream. I simply remained attentive with my eyes fixed on him, while taking in all I possibly could.

From among all the children, Neil acknowledged me with his characteristic grin and the slightest nod of his head. (He always was subtle.) Then his eyes connected with mine more intently. I could tell he knew how happy I was to see him, and how much I wanted to get closer to him. I think he could also sense my torment over being kept at arm's length from the heaven he now inhabited. Neil continued to survey the children in his care. Then he gestured toward me apologetically, showing compassion for my angst. I understood: I still had earthly work to do. Despite my longing to get nearer to my son, I accepted that I could not do so—at least, not yet. And that is how Neil and I communicated during the dream. Neil seemed to read my mind, and I seemed to understand his reactions to my thoughts!

Our exchange of thoughts continued. I registered that he was "working," and his job was to oversee and guide the children to wherever they were going. Such "work" did not seem bothersome to Neil. In fact, it did not seem like work at all. Just like the little ones, Neil was blissful; but unlike the little ones, who hadn't a care in their heavenly world, he was focused, purposeful.

Besides surmising that the serenity and order of the heavenly scene was not to be disturbed, I understood that the physical space between my deceased son and me was our only true separation. Our telepathic exchange assured me that we could still interact and communicate through our thoughts and emotions. Thus I savored every nuance of my dream.

Neil conveyed that he understood my mortal yearnings, and was sympathetic to them, yet he displayed no pity for me. His demeanor was one of understanding and reassurance. In other words, everything was in perfect order for now. Neil then diverted his attention from me and continued along with the procession of children in tow. I stood by, fully attentive and motionless, as they all passed. I strained to keep my eyes from blinking, for fear of ending the encounter. I continued to track Neil's image until he finally disappeared like a setting sun over the horizon to my left. Then, while still in my dream state, I bowed my head in gratitude. I knew the window into my son's heaven had been a gift.

Upon awakening from my dream that morning, I was not quite as grateful or accepting of what had transpired during the night. Actually, I was exhausted before my day began. Neil was nowhere in sight, and I was still confined to my earthly existence. Tears welled up from the bottom of my being. I was filled with disillusionment and distress, only magnified. Before I even had a chance to start my day, grief was there to remind me that Neil was dead. It was grief, my tormentor, who had shaken me to consciousness like the piercing clamber of a wicked alarm clock that was just out of reach. If only I could smother the obnoxious wake-up call, if only I could grasp my grief and silence it. Maybe then I could "move on." Maybe then I could be Maggie again.

Once fully conscious, I pushed grief aside and forced myself to reflect and regroup. Accepting what the dream had implied (that I had the balance of my own life to complete), I somehow needed to master grief before it mastered me. This was a spiritual battle, and one I could not win on my own. Again, I turned to God. In prayer I found my answer.

The suffering and death of God's own son, Jesus Christ, took place right in front of His human mother, Mary. This fact is so embedded in the history of mankind that scholars, theologians, artists, and sculptors have rendered masterful works based on their interpretations of the pain of this one grieving mother, a woman who was as human as the rest of us. Despite the rough edges of her own life—finding out she was an unwed mother, giving birth in a stable, watching her gentle son be condemned and crucified—she remained faithful to God's plan. By comparison, life had been kinder to me.

"Yes," I told myself, "if any spiritual figure knew my grief, it was Jesus Christ's mother, Mary—and God was her anchor through it all."

I was glad Mary's God was my God, too. I knew I would be okay. With that specific hope holding my fragile heart together, I put my dream in its place and proceeded with my day.

Dreams can be crazy or crazy-making. They can also give us information that our conscious, rational minds inhibit us from seeing. I have met dozens of other bereaved parents who have had equally detailed dreams of their own deceased children. Despite the frustration and disappointment such dreams can engender for the grieving, I behold my own like nuggets of gold and tuck them away in my memory bank of positive thoughts. Visualizing Neil among so many happy children still brings me comfort. And even today, I feel those mysterious goose bumps when I contemplate the scene. Perhaps dreams of that nature are a dose of heavenly compassion given to parents who are adjusting to the death of a child. Based on my own experience, I believe God can sneak measures of comfort, like heart stones and hopeful dreams, into any grieving family's difficult new reality.

When I shared my heavenly dream of Neil with my other kids, they could easily envision him in the capacity I had described. Neil being surrounded by children in his afterlife made sense and seemed a perfect extension of the life he had lived with them. Davin, Lauren, and Greg had always regarded Neil as an observant, engaged, and responsible big brother. In truth, he was practically unflappable amid the ups and downs of our family's busy life. But best of all, kids could be kids around Neil; he appreciated each of them for who they were—each unique, each precious.

Image 10. Davin, 10, Neil, 12 & Gregory, 17 mos. (July 1993)

Without hesitation, Neil's three siblings would snatch him right back to this life if they could. They all enjoyed remarkable relationships with their eldest brother, and I will demonstrate this in the next chapter. My purpose in doing so is to spotlight the kind of companionship young siblings must learn to live without when a brother or sister dies. My own children lost far more than a family member when Neil died. They lost an ally, a friend, a mentor, a protector, a source of laughter and joy, and an enormous measure of their security. I have no doubt that the effects of losing a sibling, especially during one's youth, are immeasurably profound.

TEN

NEIL'S THREE AMIGOS

Neil had many special relationships during his living years, but he held none more closely than those within his immediate family. For us, it is easy to credit Neil with mending our grieving hearts in a supernatural and lighthearted way. Heartifacts are uplifting and positive, just like Neil had been. Could the boy who was "too good to be true" also be too good to be gone?

I often wonder.

Neil was born reasonable and easy to love. He was careful with people and made anyone associated with him look better: his coaches, his teachers, his friends, and his relatives. Neil engaged us all with genuineness, enthusiasm, and an irrepressible sense of fun. He was interested in many things, good at most things, and humble besides. In a nutshell, Neil was a gentleman every day of his life, and we were lucky as a result.

My having a child like that as my first led me to believe that I had found my niche in life. Nothing felt more natural to me than being a mother. Thus my course was set…and then there were four: Neil and his three amigos.

Image 11. Lauren, 5, Davin, 9, Greg, 10 mos. & Neil, 11 (Christmas 1992)

Davin, another handsome little towhead, joined the Neil, Daddy, and Mommy scene in 1983. As the months and years passed, one thing became strikingly clear: my first two children were wired for vastly different experiences in life. Coming to this realization was heartbreaking. The world, which had been so perfectly suited for Neil, was an obstacle course for Davin. *Nothing* came easily for my second child. Life seemed to throw one hurdle up after another for Neil's first amigo.

Lovable and endearing as he was, there was no clear-cut path for how to best support my second child. Consequently, every member of our family faced new challenges. Together we celebrated the little guy's hard-earned successes and suffered his confounding challenges. It was an unexpectedly confusing time.

For a child who was only two years older than his first sibling, Neil was an instinctively patient, protective, and compassionate big brother. In the most uncomplicated ways, Neil made a positive difference in his little brother's life. Davin could not have had a better guardian, role model, or buddy than Neil. He was Davin's best friend.

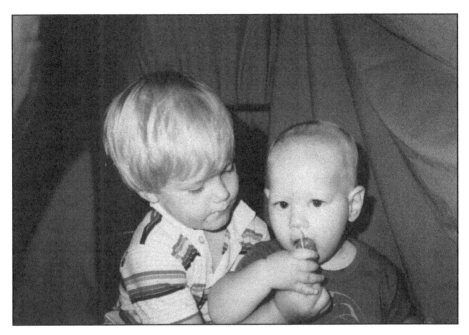

Image 12. Fort building, popsicles & brotherly love; Neil, 3 & Davin, 1 (Summer 1984)

A textbook example of Neil's role in Davin's life occurred on Halloween night in 1990. We had just moved into a new neighborhood, and the boys were nine and seven years old, respectively. Before long, something amazing came to our attention: Mario Lemieux lived within a half mile of our new house. Though still in his twenties, the Canadian ice hockey phenomenon was well on his way to becoming legendary, not only among Pittsburgh Penguin fans but throughout the world of athletics.

Pittsburgh loves its professional athletes, and young Mario, like my Neil, was easy to love. History reveals that the feeling between Pittsburgh and Mario was probably mutual. During the 1980s, Mr. Lemieux adopted our city as his own. This fact delighted Pittsburghers of all ages, including Neil. He could not believe his good fortune as Halloween approached; with any luck, Neil would get to meet his new neighbor, Mario Lemieux, in person!

The opportunity to trick or treat at Lemieux's residence was something few children in the area passed up. In fact, it drew kids from well beyond our neighborhood. Like droves of other young fans, Neil could not wait; Mario had already won a Stanley Cup, the trophy awarded to the best of the best in the professional hockey world. Kids like Neil idolized him.

As the October sun set and darkness rolled in, I put the finishing touches on my children's costumes. The boys were heading out for tricks and treats. Two-year-old Lauren and I remained home to distribute candy to the witches, warlocks, werewolves, and superheroes that rang our front doorbell. All three of my children were revved, but Neil even more so.

My eldest had a Halloween strategy, and he shared it with his dad and Davin just before they headed out. First, the boys would canvas Main Entrance Drive for treats, and then circle back to Lebanon Hills Drive via Park Entrance. From there, they would head south, and then make the left onto Mario Lemieux's street. His house was the white brick one located about a block and a half down Lynn Haven Drive, on the right-hand side. The neighborhood boys had pointed Mario's house out to Neil long before Halloween night arrived. He knew he would recognize it by the distinctive stone wall that trimmed the property and led up to the front door. Neil could hardly wait to get started. The treat of meeting Mario Lemieux was bound to create a memory that would last a lifetime.

What could be better? Well, we would see.

For Davin, who did not embrace athletics nor have any natural enthusiasm for sports, meeting Mario Lemieux or any other athlete meant very little. Sports were challenging and disappointing ventures for a child like Davin. Whether he attempted to be a participant or a spectator, they represented nothing but stress to him. But trick or treating was right up Davin's alley. Following Neil's lead, off he and Dad went.

When the trio reached Mario's white provincial house, my two little goblins peeled off from their dad, disappeared behind the landmark wall, and hustled up the driveway to Mr. Lemieux's front door. Neil was anxiously excited. Once they reached the front stoop, he took a deep breath, collected himself, and pointed to the doorbell. That was Davin's cue to push the button. He enjoyed the younger-sibling privilege of ringing for the homeowners. Meanwhile, as he later reported, Neil had butterflies rumbling in his stomach.

As someone began to turn the doorknob from the inside, both boys braced themselves. The movement of the handle was their "ready, set" signal. Then, when the huge front door finally swung open, Neil and Davin shouted, "Trick or treat!" in unison.

Neil could hardly believe it! There he was, face-to-face with Mario Lemieux, who was accompanied by his pretty Nathalie.

"It was so awesome, Mom!" Neil assured me later that night.

Then he and Davin accepted candy bars from the handsome couple and responded with a well-rehearsed, "Thank you!"

So far, so good…or so Neil thought.

Suddenly, *Davin launched himself directly into Le Magnifique's house!* And Neil's once-in-a-lifetime moment fizzled like an expended firework. Yep, his little brother whizzed himself right past Mario and Nathalie as if he were a human hockey puck! The host and hostess were probably taken aback at this, but Neil was dumbstruck. Davin had crossed the line this time—*literally!*

"How in the world did Davin catch Mario Lemieux off guard?" Neil later asked me incredulously.

But when it actually happened, Neil remained properly planted right where Davin had left him: *outside* Mario's front door. Neil's mind must have been shrieking, "No, Davin! Nooo!", for the elder brother was mortified.

Not Davin, though; he was elated! He had taken aim at his target and had hit the bull's eye that night.

Neil was the first to notice what Davin had gone after with such fervor, but Nathalie and Mario caught on quickly. The younger brother wanted to pet their dog. Truthfully, Davin was a fan of dogs as much as Neil was a fan of Mario Lemieux and the Pittsburgh Penguins. Once he noticed the pup during the Halloween treat handoff, getting nearer to it was suddenly all that mattered to him.

Flabbergasted, Neil remained fixed, frozen.

All means did not typically justify an end where Neil was concerned. But for Davin, the opposite often seemed to be true. He processed life from a unique perspective and unwittingly caught plenty of people off guard along the way. Most times his proclivities were harmless, if not comical, but his methods for achieving the outcome he sought were sometimes challenging for others.

On the night of the infamous Halloween surprise, Neil specifically remarked, "There was no way I was going inside Mario Lemieux's house! When Davin ran in there, Mom, all I wanted to do was disappear!"

My eldest had no idea how to correct the situation, but the host and hostess put their heads together and a resolution came about naturally. The couple gently guided their little intruder back to Neil within moments, and Davin's faux pas was rectified. Meanwhile, forever had come and gone for Neil. Together the boys then retraced their steps down Lemieux's driveway and toward the sidewalk where their father was waiting. Once arriving there, Neil could finally exhale.

When Neil finished sharing all of this, I smiled and suggested the following to him: "Well, if Mario Lemieux can control a speeding hockey puck for a living, he probably didn't mind redirecting your little brother this evening. He is far less threatening! Besides, Davin was probably putty in Nathalie's hands; he cannot resist a pretty girl."

Neil did not really see the humor in my reasoning. He was just glad the embarrassing moment was over. Thankfully, the Lemieuxs' instincts concerning both of my boys were golden.

When my guys returned home that Halloween night, I knew something unusual had occurred the minute I saw Neil's face. Normally, unloading his cache of treats—in a single "abracadabra" motion—was the usual big finish. But when he rattled off every detail of what I have just told you, his exasperated expression made sense; Neil had a lot to get off his chest! But in the end, it turned out to be a very good Halloween for both my boys—despite the spontaneous and unintentional "trick" Davin had interjected into the evening.

For Neil, meeting Mario Lemieux in person was awesome! When Mr. Lemieux answered his door, and then handed Neil a Halloween treat, the dream my nine-year-old son imagined had indeed come true. For this, he felt very lucky. And we all know that Davin had a good time! It really had been an extra special night for both of my boys.

It could not have been easy to call forth the patience and composure Neil demonstrated when he was so mercilessly caught off-guard. But that was Neil: a natural with younger kids and a rock for his siblings. He exercised compassion, love, and good sense where any of them were concerned.

Believe it or not, the boy-meets-hero story between Neil and Mario Lemieux did not end on October 31, 1990. A sequel arose nine years later, but for a very different reason. Mario had been advised of Neil's diagnosis of Ewing's sarcoma by a friend of mine. On December 13, 1999, the two met as adults. Neil was eighteen and about halfway through his cancer treatments when the unexpected invitation arrived.

Mario and Nathalie Lemieux reached out to cancer victims often, but they had no reason to connect teenage Neil with a child who had once trick-or-treated at the front door of their previous home. The night that was so memorable to us was probably tangential to them; dozens if not hundreds of Halloween masqueraders knocked at the Lemieuxs' front door annually.

When the news of Neil's shocking diagnosis reached my lifelong friend, Lisa Pompeani, and her husband, Bob, they both wanted to do something special for Neil. So many people did. Bob happened to be a professional sportscaster in Pittsburgh. Consequently, he and Lisa had developed many strong friendships with other local celebrities, including many of Pittsburgh's professional athletes. Mario and Nathalie Lemieux were among the closest of the Pompeanis' such friends. After speaking to me personally, Bob and Lisa felt they knew just what to do for Neil, a true fan of the Pittsburgh Penguins.

Bob and Lisa placed a call to Penguin #66 on Neil's behalf. Their plan was to procure a Mario-signed Penguin hockey jersey or stick for Neil. They felt that either gift might lift my son's spirit as he confronted his life-threatening disease. When my friends finally shared their intentions with me, I felt that *any* expression of encouragement from Mario Lemieux would inspire Neil in an especially significant way. Mario knew cancer firsthand. He had survived Hodgkin's lymphoma since starting his hockey career in Pittsburgh. I knew it, and I am sure Neil knew it. (If you lived in Pittsburgh, it would have been hard not to know it.) I felt Mario could truly identify with Neil, and I appreciated what Lisa and Bob had suggested. When they approached Mario and explained Neil's treacherous situation to him, Mr. Lemieux responded compassionately. The Pompeanis knew he would. Mario always came through.

I waited to see what would unfold.

Lisa filled me in. Mario had indeed promised to provide some signed memorabilia for Neil, but that was not all he had in mind. Out of respect for the lifelong friendship Lisa and I shared, he wanted to do something more; he wanted to meet Neil personally, but not at the hospital. He wanted Neil to be comfortable and thought a less clinical setting would promote ease for my son. Mario's idea for Neil took many people by surprise. After working the details out with Children's Hospital, the Penguin's plan was privately unveiled.

Mr. and Mrs. Lemieux ended up inviting Neil and four other pediatric oncology patients to their home for dinner. The only stipulation was that each youngster be accompanied by a registered nurse. The coordinators from the hospital had no trouble rounding up five volunteers; an invitation like that was akin to Cinderella being invited to the royal ball!

As Neil prepared for his second audience with the Lemieuxs, I ribbed him (gently) about the first.

Eighteen-year-old Neil promptly replied, "I don't think I will be reminding them that I trick-or-treated at their previous home in 1990, Mom."

Neil felt very fortunate to be getting another chance to meet Mario and Nathalie Lemieux. But this time, he hoped to avoid any embarrassing surprises. He was very excited and appreciative for the new opportunity as it approached. It was a pinnacle example of the warmness and caring being extended toward him from so many sources. Pittsburghers really rally for one of their own. Ours is a big city with a small-town heart.

On the night of the event, Neil and the other nine guests convened at the main entrance to Children's Hospital. From there, they were transported to the Lemieux estate by limousine.

"Mario, Nathalie, and their children greeted us as if we were royalty, Mom," Neil exclaimed to me after the affair. Of course, he also reminded me that Mario was reputed to be a class act.

Much to Neil's delight, he learned that Mario had even summoned his favorite chef to create an unforgettable gourmet meal for the special guests to feast upon.

"While dinner preparations were being finalized, Mario and Nathalie toured all of us through their incredible home," he reported afterward. "A few of us could not help but laugh when we noticed crayon drawings in one of their stairways, Mom. It made Mario's family seem more like the rest of ours."

To top everything off, when dinner was served, each boy's place around the formal dining table was adorned with a personalized Penguin jersey, a Mario Lemieux biography, and an official NHL hockey puck—all signed by Mario!

Everything was perfect!

When Neil's cohort and their nurses finally returned to Children's Hospital that evening, the other parents and I waited anxiously as the limousine approached. None of us could wait to hear about the evening our boys had spent with the local sports legend they adored. But before Neil ever got to me with his own impressions, one of the nurses sought me out and pulled me aside. At first, I was a little nervous. Then I learned that Neil's escort was excited to tell me something that Mrs. Lemieux had shared with her when the group first arrived at the Sewickley home.

"Just as your son and I entered the Lemieuxs' house, Nathalie took one look at Neil and appeared to be taken aback," she said. "Then, out of his earshot, she whispered to me, 'The boy you're with looks just like my young Mario!'"

I smiled at the nurse and told her how crazy it was that Nathalie Lemieux had made that particular observation; several other people, including total strangers, had recently made similar comments to me about Neil's resemblance to her husband. Mrs. Lemieux's assertion surely confirmed what I had been hearing. I am reminded of her unsolicited, affirming remark whenever I see images and videos of her husband, Mario. It is comforting for me to see traces of Neil in someone so highly regarded and admired. It even seems fitting.

As Neil and I returned home that night, he was clearly grateful for the experience he had shared with Mario Lemieux and his family. In jest, I asked Neil if it was an improvement upon his first meeting them on Halloween in 1990. He chuckled affirmatively, but in a subdued manner.

I sensed the wheels turning in Neil's mind. Suddenly I understood his restraint.

Even though Neil's first meeting with the Lemieuxs had not gone perfectly, at least he was a carefree little boy at the time (well, *mostly* carefree). Back then, our family was intact and Neil did not have cancer. So much had happened during the years since, and Neil seemed to be processing all of it. I so wished I could fix everything for him. I continued driving and adjusted my level of enthusiasm accordingly. A few minutes later I broke the silence in the car by asking just one more question.

"What was your favorite memory of tonight's visit with the Lemieuxs?"

Neil replied softly, but without hesitation, "Seeing Mario with his family was the best thing of all. His trophy room was amazing, but it was just as cool to see him being a dad. His little boy even pitched a fit when he was told it was time for bed. Mario wasn't upset or embarrassed; he just laughed, 'cause it was funny!"

Neil's reply was not really what I expected to hear, but it was very true to the Neil I knew. I painted a mental picture, grinned about what Neil had told me, and drove on.

I admired Neil so much. He was *never* confused about the things that mattered most in life. I was very, very grateful to be his mom.

Image 13. Mario Lemieux & Neil (December 1999)

Starting with the birth of his first sibling, Neil revered his role as a big brother and handled the associated responsibilities better than any. The addition of a sister and a second brother enhanced his brilliance in that role even more. Looking back, I now feel certain that Neil had more in common with Mario Lemieux than looks alone. Both superstars could be counted on, neither shrunk in the face of adversity, and both gave more than anyone ever expected.

Neil's little sister, Lauren, entered his world on January 9, 1988. These two shared an instinctive bond, and it was obvious from the moment I first placed her in his arms. Although he was only six and a half years old, Neil cradled his newborn sister as if he had done it a thousand times before. In turn, his new amiga, Lauren, snuggled into her eldest brother's arms as if she belonged there. It was a true privilege to watch their bond get ever stronger through the years they shared. Neil and Lauren were kindred spirits and sparkled in each other's company.

**Image 14. Neil, 6, meeting baby Lauren, 5 days,
with Mommy (January 14, 1988)**

In no time, dainty Lauren's bright and happy disposition emerged. There was nothing dainty about her spirit, though. By the time she was a toddler, it was clear she was capable, independent, and slightly fearless. Having two older brothers may have contributed to these aspects of her nature. Lauren carved out her unique niche in the family, bringing positive energy and a special balance to the dynamic of the entire group.

Shortly after Lauren turned four, a new baby brother was also on board. Gregory was born on February 11, 1992, following a long winter and tenuous pregnancy. To celebrate his arrival and good health, we took a family trip seven weeks later. Our goal was to unwind and recover from the concerns that had been wearing on us throughout the pregnancy. The six of us piled into our minivan and headed to State College—the town nestled against my college alma mater in the mountains of Central Pennsylvania. For many years, we had regarded the main campus of Penn State University and the surrounding area as our home away from home.

After the four-hour drive, we checked in at our hotel. We were all anxious to get our weekend of fun and relaxation underway. To that end, the three older children pointed out the indoor pool near the hotel's lobby. They were elated with the idea of swimming that day. It had been a *long* winter. The baby didn't need a swim, however; he needed to be fed and get horizontal—the infant car seat had cramped Gregory's style! To appease everyone, my husband and I decided to divide and conquer. He accompanied Neil, Davin, and Lauren to the pool, while I headed to the elevator and up to our room with Greg.

I had barely gotten the baby down for his much-needed nap when the phone in our room rang. The call was from a front desk attendant in the hotel lobby. Politely, he requested that I come down to the aquatics room.

When I asked him for an explanation, he calmly said, "Your daughter needs you."

I questioned him further, since I had just gotten Gregory to sleep.

The caller replied with more urgency, "There has been an accident involving your daughter at the pool."

I reacted immediately, scooping Greg up and heading for the elevator. On my way down to the lobby, I convinced myself that my excited four-year-old had probably slipped and fallen on the wet tile around the pool. I expected to find Lauren crying while holding a bag of ice on her head. The scene I actually walked in on was much worse. My normally lively little Lauren lay motionless and blue at the poolside. She was not breathing.

Had Greg not been in my arms, I might have gotten hysterical. Instead, I scanned the group gathered around her and asked, "Why isn't anyone helping her? Has an ambulance been called?"

A shocked crowd stared blankly back at me. It included the hotel manager, a lifeguard, an exercise instructor (with her adult students), ten-year-old Neil, eight-year-old Davin, and my husband. Every one of them was in shock!

Surely someone standing there frozen with fear had been trained in cardiopulmonary resuscitation (CPR), I thought. They had to be! I knew the jobs of at least three of them would have required such certification.

"Oh no," I asked myself, "do they think Lauren is already dead?"

I was scared, but I could not panic. I had been trained in CPR shortly after Neil was born, and the time had come to use it. Ten years had passed since then, so my mind offered up a split-second prayer that I would remember what I had learned. As I took a step closer to Lauren, I also wondered how long she had been in that helpless condition. I motioned toward someone to take Gregory from my arms.

Simultaneously, Lauren's father knelt down and gently placed his hand on her distended belly. I do not know what prompted him to do just that, just then; but his instincts to do so were perfect. With the force of a volcanic eruption, Lauren began vomiting what seemed like gallons of fluid from her tiny body. There were cheers and tears of relief at seeing her suddenly conscious.

In the background, the sirens of an approaching ambulance blared. I was relieved and still amazed by what had just taken place. Lauren's father had no rescue training whatsoever, yet he had delivered healing to his little girl's lifeless body. To this day, I am thankful that his touch revived her. Perhaps it triggered some physiological reflex in Lauren's bloated little body, but I still wonder if something less clinical had stepped in. It certainly seemed so. When Lauren returned to consciousness so unexpectedly, several of us standing there felt as if we had just witnessed a miracle.

Paramedics joined the scene and did a preliminary assessment of my young daughter's condition. Although she seemed fully recovered from the near drowning, I soon learned that no one knew how long Lauren had been unable to breathe. Had the four critical minutes of oxygen deprivation passed after which brain damage often occurs? Although Lauren being alive at all seemed miraculous, she was not out of the woods. Doctors had to determine whether or not she had suffered brain damage from the episode. The ambulance crew promptly transported Lauren to Centre County Community Hospital for further evaluation.

The emergency room specialists were prepared for Lauren's arrival by ambulance, and they examined her immediately. Upon their completion of the appropriate medical and neurological tests, they reported their findings to my husband and me. Lauren had dodged a proverbial bullet and exhibited no signs of permanent damage.

Hallelujah! Lauren had come away from a nearly fatal pool accident with no residual effects. It seemed unbelievable! Everyone among us was so grateful. In my own mind, I was on my knees. God had indeed spared little Lauren that day.

Still, my head was spinning.

Attending to Lauren's medical condition had been the first order of business when all of us arrived at the hospital. But after the crisis had passed and we knew she was all right, a multitude of questions flooded my mind. As a family, we all wanted to put the horror of Lauren's near drowning behind us, but I also needed to process the haunting events that nearly took my little girl's life. I mean, my cherished daughter nearly died that afternoon! One or two questions to Neil later that day filled in surprising details that were nearly as astounding as Lauren's recovery.

Specifically, I asked Neil how he was holding up after witnessing such a horrifying turn of events. In response to my query, tears welled up in his eyes. That alone told me that he had observed more during the traumatic pool episode than I had realized. I acknowledged his discomfort and tried to console him, but the ten-year-old dismissed any concern directed at him. All he wanted from me was assurance that Lauren was completely fine. After I provided as much, he then offered several alarming details.

Neil was swimming with Davin in the pool's deep end, when he first noticed that Lauren was not on the deck of the pool where he had last seen her. After scanning the room, he was shocked to see her at the opposite end of the pool, facedown in the shallow water. He got to his little sister as fast as he could and rolled her over immediately. To his horror, Lauren was bloated, her skin was blue, and she appeared to be lifeless. Wasting no time, Neil gathered her up, carried her to the side of the pool, and laid her on its deck, which is precisely where she was when I arrived at the dreadful scene. To learn that it was Neil who first responded to Lauren left me speechless for several moments.

When I integrated the missing pieces of the pool disaster into the whole terrifying story, I was in complete awe of Neil's courage and maturity. I always knew I had been spoiled by this child, whose instincts seemed to align with what was best for our family at every turn. Following Lauren's near drowning, however, I felt Neil was much more than observant and heroic; to me he was angelic (or, at least, guided to behave angelically). Considering his age and his sister's condition, his quiet and decisive actions that afternoon were profound. Nothing in his ten years of life had prepared him for the extreme situation. Blessedly, my watchful firstborn had his little sister's back that day. Upon reflection, Neil usually had somebody's back (whether or not that person was aware of it). It was another facet of his extraordinary nature.

**Image 15. Lauren, 4, Neil, 10 & Davin, 8, at Beaver Stadium
(Penn State University, University Park, PA, March 1992)**

Neil's influence upon his siblings expanded even further as the youngest, Gregory, outgrew his infancy. He gave Neil plenty of opportunities to stretch his big-brother wings, too. Gregory, Amigo Number Three, was a powerful force in our family from early on. For this reason, Neil affectionately dubbed him "the Factor" by the time he was only two years old. The nickname was short for "the Greg Factor."

To quote Neil: "There was life as we knew it, before Greg. Then there was life with the ever-exciting Greg factored in." Neil made this observation as if his life as the eldest of my children had previously been a breeze!

"The Factor" was not the first nickname for our robust and alert Gregory, though. There were people calling my brand-new baby "Bubba" before he left the obstetrical unit where he was born. It was a reflection of his size compared to that of the other newborns in the hospital's nursery. As the Factor/Bubba continued to develop, he lived up to both monikers. Together, they embodied his personality and his superhero physicality. By the time Greg was a toddler, twelve-year-old Neil had simply accepted his little brother's GI Joe attitude and physique.

At the time, my emerging teenager had even inquired, "Hey, Mom, how did Greg get the six-pack *I've* been working on?"

Neil was observant and funny; his query made us both laugh. He and I also knew that Greg's formidable appearance was only dwarfed by his fearless personality. On one hand, my eldest son was proud of his "bad-ass" little brother. On the other, Neil affectionately envied the Factor for his God-given muscularity. Well, the caboose of our family made use of his "Factor" status and lived most of his formative years as if he were on one death-defying mission or another. I later learned the basis for his modus operandi.

In preparation for this chapter, Greg and I discussed various aspects of his nine years with Neil. Greg had no trouble expressing what Neil meant to him. He emulated his older brother and shared as many of his interests as he could. One in particular was a fascination with James Bond, Secret Agent 007. Bond was a fictional spy known for executing highly technical daredevil stunts during his quest to save lives and solve mysteries involving international espionage. The character's ultra-macho persona appealed to men and women alike.

Greg, of course, admired James Bond films from a kid's point of view during the nineties. And the seven-year-old had been paying closer attention to 007 than anyone at home had realized! Being exposed to Bond's mystique quietly fueled Greg's inborn lust for adventure; thus the Factor became even more of a factor for Neil. But, as Greg's following remark attests, enjoying spy films together was only a sliver of the brotherly relationship he and Neil enjoyed:

"Maybe you should tell your readers about how Neil used to take me four-wheeling in his stripped-down Jeep Wrangler, and then follow it up with a trip to Red Lobster on all-you-can-eat king crab leg night. We ate those things like there was no tomorrow!"

Ironic choice of words, I thought to myself. Then I shot him a look that said, "You have got to be kidding."

He grinned broadly, knowing I needed something a little more substantive for the purposes of this book. He recollected further.

"How about the time Neil rescued me from my self-designed bungee jump? I think I was seven years old."

I silently recalled the incident, shuddering at the memory, and asked him to continue.

"I remember desperately wanting to bungee jump, only I didn't have a bungee cord. Truthfully, I don't think I had ever even seen one in real life," Gregory added.

For the record, a true bungee cord is an elasticized line with a clasp at each end. It is typically used as a fastener. The sport of bungee jumping involves attaching oneself to a high structure with a heavy-gauge bungee cord, and then jumping off. The jumper's goal is to *safely* experience free fall without hitting the surface below. In other words, it is intended to be exhilarating and harmless fun. I suspect James Bond was adept at bungee jumping!

Lacking an authentic bungee cord, my young adventurer searched and searched our house for a rope instead. (And because he was acting undercover, he never sought help during his quest.) Greg's rope search was no more productive than his bungee search had been. Still, the young Bond protégé did not waiver from his mission. His tenacity finally led him to my laundry room catch-all drawer, where he discovered a handful of shoelaces and drawstrings. It represented the mother lode of lines and spawned a new solution for his bungee-cord dilemma. The Factor's determination, creativity, and resourcefulness aligned just then, and he proceeded to manufacture his own bungee cord. Greg tied the hodgepodge of laces and strings together, end to end.

Once the bits of cord had been connected, Greg spied his launch site: the ten-foot-high basketball hoop above the garage door. Its obscure location on the side of the house was perfect from my secret-agent wannabe's perspective. He could carry out his covert mission without being noticed.

Connecting the makeshift bungee cord to the hoop six feet above his head became Greg's next challenge. With sheer determination, the child dragged an extension ladder from the garage and leaned it up against the house by himself! How he ever accomplished this feat without drawing anyone's attention still baffles me. Greg was a stealthy youngster—very Bondesque.

After climbing the ladder, Greg secured one end of his special rope to the rim of the hoop and the other around his waist. Using all of his might, he then made stringent tugs on the line to test its integrity. Once he felt certain that his unique bungee cord would bear his weight, he concluded that all systems were go. With jump time at hand, Greg then kicked the ladder out from under himself! It crashed to the ground along a trajectory that sent it away from the house altogether.

Unfortunately, Greg soon learned that all systems had definitely not been go.

Two distinct problems had arisen during his maiden bungee jump, which halted abruptly as a result. First of all, the homemade line was not elasticized; therefore, it had no buoyancy and became taut when he jumped. Secondly, he had fastened the cord around his waist with a slipknot, whereby he was left to dangle about five feet above our asphalt driveway with a hangman's noose around his waist! Greg's torso was literally being strangled! In that condition, the Factor hung helplessly and weighed his options.

The ladder, which now lay upon the ground, had become useless to him. Plus, he could hardly breathe while being cinched about the waist. Besides the discomfort, this fact made calling for help nearly impossible. The only good news for Greg was that his homemade bungee cord had held his weight and prevented him from crashing into the pavement below.

"Ouch!" my grown Greg grunted. "Did I ever feel stupid hanging there like that! Can you believe I was actually more embarrassed than panicky, Mom?"

Then he added, "Finally, I just barely squeaked out, 'Help!' It was so lame, but it was the best I could do."

"Bond never would have been so shortsighted," my full-grown Factor finally confessed. He looked to the ground, snickering in disbelief and shaking his head at the close call he had actually survived.

Well, the universe must have been on Greg's side that day; Neil heard the faint, raspy plea he had choked out. After following Greg's subdued cry through our foyer, Neil opened the interior door to see his little brother hanging in the double-wide garage door opening. Neil called for me instantly and bolted toward Greg. As I galloped down the staircase to the foyer, I glanced into the garage and could not believe the predicament Greg had gotten himself into! Neil looked back at me just as perplexed, and I thanked God for him—again.

When I joined the pair, Neil was standing as tall as he could with both of his arms wrapped firmly around Gregory's legs. Neil had instinctively lifted his youngest brother enough to get his weight off the line, but the loop around Greg's belly was still snug. I loosened the noose by hand as best I could, but had to leave the boys momentarily to get scissors. The only way to sufficiently free Greg from the dangerous nonbungee cord was to cut it. All the while, Neil kept Greg aloft and safe from further harm.

After Greg was out of danger and finally on solid ground again, the three of us exhaled. We were all relieved that things hadn't turned out much, much worse. Then Neil and I looked at each other while fighting back the kind of laughter that might have turned into tears. Meanwhile Gregory "the Factor" Bond didn't know whether to laugh or cry. Instead he grumbled under his breath about his humiliating mishap. Neil winked at me, sensing his little brother's embarrassment, but he did not rub Greg's nose in his folly. Instead, he lifted him into the topless, doorless Jeep Wrangler, and the boys took off for burgers and Cokes.

Everything made those two hungry!

Image 16. Greg, 8 & Neil, 18, at Mt. Lebanon HS graduation (June 1999)

Since then, the Factor has grown to be as handsome and strong as Neil had been before his illness. Gregory is now a young adult who looks a lot like his eldest brother and exhibits many of Neil's mannerisms. As a result, I refer to Greg by Neil's name way too often. The grown-up Factor accepts my mistakes with a certain amount of pride, realizing they are tricks of my subconscious. I know I am forgiven when he responds to my mistake by lobbing an acquiescing half-smile in my direction, an expression so reminiscent of Neil.

Greg actually loves being mistaken for a brother he remembers with utmost admiration. Despite having been barely ten years old when Neil died, Greg did his best to fill the big shoes Neil left behind. When that devastating loss occurred, my youngest became the second self-proclaimed protector of my shrinking family. Neil, of course, was the first.

Life as the eldest of my children was a tall order, and Neil was masterful in that position. He was naturally attentive and good-natured, and took every day in stride—even during his illness. Since his passing, Neil continues to inspire our family as well as countless other people. In many instances, the appearance of a heartifact validates what we already feel intuitively.

Neil's spirit is an active one, especially in relation to people with whom he felt especially close. His cousin, Megan, is one of those people. Toward the end of his life, she became particularly important to Neil. Megan was there when the going got tough for him and the rest of us. She held each of my children together at one time or another. And once Neil required all of my attention, she held me up, too. As you will see, Neil has not forgotten Megan's unconditional dedication to his family. And she has plenty of her own heartifacts to prove it.

ELEVEN

HEARTS FOR MEGAN

It is difficult to single out anyone who came to my family's aid between 1998 and 2001. We relied on so many caring people during that period that it is humbling. But for reasons I think you will understand, I must elaborate on my niece Megan's contributions. She was critical in reinforcing my destabilized family during that most ruinous time period. In November of 2000, Megan showed up like Joan of Arc when, after a teasing recovery, Neil's cancer returned in merciless fashion.

Megan was the second woman who had filtered into my household to support Davin, Lauren, and Greg while I focused on Neil and his resurgent medical needs. Stepping into the dynamic of my group was no easy task. Eight-year-old Greg showed his appreciation by promptly labeling Megan his "worstest" nightmare. She laughed and considered it a badge of honor—she had trumped her predecessor! After all, my dear friend, Sally, had only achieved "worst" nightmare status during her stay with us. On the contrary, both women were indispensable to me and my children as we adjusted to Neil's critical setback.

Megan's role morphed as suddenly as Neil's cancer had returned. When that happened, she shifted from being a nanny for my three younger children to administering hospice care to Neil. Neither job was a joyride, but Megan's resolve to help us was unshakeable. I do not know what we would have done without her. She cared for her dying cousin, and she supported me as I supported him. Megan's compassion and courage always preceded her own needs. Ultimately, Neil's declining health required twenty-seven-year-old Megan to be "on call" around the clock. A weaker person would have run in the opposite direction.

What Megan did for us was a major detour from her Smoky Mountain lifestyle and her work as a river guide in Hartford, Tennessee. She therefore processed the sad and draining experience we had all shared for about a year before returning to river-running in the environs she loved. Megan finally reunited with her whitewater "family" in April of 2002.

Once returning to Hartford, Megan wasted no time in getting to the river. She and her friends decided to mark her return with an early spring rafting run on the Pigeon. As usual, there was no better place to meet than at the put-in near the hydroelectric power plant. It was the traditional launch site for all of her group's whitewater excursions. But when Megan approached the put-in, she was stunned; she saw something new and surprising—something that had not been there when she headed north to support my children and me during the previous year.

A *huge* patch of erosion was now apparent on the concrete retaining wall attached to the power plant. And it was shaped like a heart! Megan could not miss it. No one could miss it. This new heart in Hartford was even larger than the sport utility vehicle on the parking deck above it!

If Megan had ever thought that my heart tales were a mere symptom of my grief, the in-your-face heart that greeted her at the Pigeon

River put-in caused her to reconsider. Her very own eyes saw and intuition told her (independent of me) that there was a connection between Neil and the hearts showing up for his loved ones since his passing. Megan was happy to report her surprising discovery to me.

For a couple of reasons I was delighted to hear that a heartifact had emerged especially for Megan: First of all, she had certainly earned one! Secondly, the put-in heart objectively reinforced the phenomenon my children and I had been enjoying during the previous year. As you know, I had been somewhat guarded about the unusual trend at first. But time and experiences, like this one concerning Megan, kept reminding me that heartifacts were not coincidental; they were amazing!

**Image 17. Davin, 19 & Megan, 28, at Pigeon River
put-in (Tennessee, summer 2002)**

I don't know how many nights I spent tossing and turning over the mysterious hearts that kept showing up. I even wondered if I was just a grieving mother trying to convince herself that any good could come from accepting the loss of her child. Invariably, however, I was soon welcoming another heart to my collection, or at least a photograph of it! Not everyone in my life had been enchanted with what was occurring, however.

My own father once said to me, "Face it, Margaret, death is death."

Instead of debating my father about his "death is death" proclamation, I casually replied, "I could not get out of bed every morning if I had to face Greg, Lauren, and Davin with such an attitude, Dad. They need encouragement and whatever hope they can muster. They have already lost their stable family, their grandmother, their big brother, and probably trust in anything. I will not take away their hope of healing from all of these tragedies. The hearts we have gathered bring us hope. The hearts are part of our healing."

To think of death as nothing more than an ending had no place in my world, especially since finding my original heart stone in Carlsbad, California. Thanks to the new heart in Tennessee, my niece, Megan, was one family member who was starting to get the picture.

I felt so blessed when Megan made herself available to assist my children and me during Neil's struggles with cancer. The circumstances we shared and the lessons we learned through the process were dramatically life-altering. The entire experience pointed both of us in directions we might never have considered previously. Several years after Neil died, I was encouraged to speak and write about how my children and I had survived grief. As for Megan, she grew from being a Pigeon River rafting guide before Neil's illness, to becoming a full-time hospice nurse in Knoxville, Tennessee, after his death.

Megan credits Neil with planting the seeds of this dramatic change in her life, but she did her part, too. Megan's determination and giving nature are what really brought life to her goal of supporting the critically ill through their transitions from this life. I witnessed this firsthand when physical healing was no longer a realistic goal for Neil; Megan had adjusted to his needs, and mine, almost instinctively. She helped both of us as Neil prepared for his ultimate journey. When that time came, another kind of caring and healing was needed, and Megan instinctively provided both. Her dedication to my children and me still inspires us.

While training rigorously for her new career, Megan still made time to retreat to nature for restoration and renewal. The mountains and rivers of Tennessee provided all that she needed to maintain a healthy balance in her new life. During that process, Megan fell in love with more than her surroundings; she met Huck, who is now her husband. They planned for a wedding along the river they adored, and most of the clan joined them for the joyous celebration.

On August 1, 2010, Davin and I joined at least a hundred other wedding guests at a picnic grove near the banks of the Pigeon River. We were all awaiting the arrival of the bridal couple. During this waiting period, I drifted deep into thought about my very special niece and all that she had done for my immediate family when our world was under siege. As a follow-up to those musings, I stepped away from the crowd, dug a pen and a scrap of paper out of my purse, and earnestly attempted to compose a toast to honor her. I hoped to share it during the wedding reception.

After a short while, Davin joined me. He could tell by my watery eyes that I had been struggling with my endeavor. In the end, I decided I could not translate my feelings about my beautiful niece into a toast; it would end up being too emotional and probably inadequate. The gratitude and admiration I have for Megan is inexplicable. I realized then and there that her wedding day was not the appropriate time to expound.

I abandoned my notion of writing the toast and asked Davin if he would join me for a short walk. My gentle companion obliged. It was clear to him that I needed to regroup and get into the right frame of mind for the happy event about to take place. We wandered away from the other guests at the picnic grove and headed toward the bank of the river. As usual, I gravitated straight toward the water for comfort. There, I knew I could pull myself together.

With no particular forethought, I kicked my sandals off at the water's edge and invited Davin to do the same. Next, I stepped into the ankle-deep water and felt refreshed immediately. As usual, nearby river rocks caught my attention and got me thinking of Neil. I even joked about it to Davin as he continued to untie his shoes.

I then asked him, "Wouldn't *now* be a perfect time for Neil to come through with a heart rock for Megan and Huck? I mean, a heartifact from Neil would be much more meaningful than a sappy toast from me."

Davin, now barefoot, nodded at me in quiet agreement.

Meanwhile, I took one more step in the water, and it was a step that caused me to stop dead in my tracks. At that exact moment, I thought I spotted a heart rock on the floor of the sandy riverbed. Even I was skeptical, but I reached forward to pick up the rock anyway, knowing it was the only way to find out if the shimmering of the water was playing tricks on my eyes.

"Could I just be observing the distortion of an ordinary rock?" I wondered, as my hand entered the water to grasp the stone. "Do I just *want* to see a heart rock right now?"

As I lifted the specimen out of the water, I pronounced, "It can't be!"

I turned to my son. "I just found another heart rock, Davin! And this one is the real deal. I can't believe it!"

Sunlight illuminated the new and undeniable heartifact I balanced in my hand. I was delighted; it was substantial and it was perfect.

"Thank you, Neil," was all I could say.

As I climbed ashore, I murmured, "Yes!"

Image 18. Megan, Maggie & Pigeon River heartifact (August 2010)

Had Davin not been my witness, no one would have believed that I stumbled upon a heart rock for Megan and Huck that very day. Even more astounding was our being led back to the very same spot on the river bank for the wedding service only an hour later! The minister stood *exactly* where I had entered the water and found Megan and Huck's wedding heartifact. I was floored by this, even though I had to keep it to myself until after the service concluded. I was filled with joy for the couple and for myself; I felt Neil was in our midst.

Shortly after their nuptials, I found an opportunity to give the supernatural gift to the newlyweds. At first, Huck and Megan assumed that I had chosen their heart rock from my collection back in Pittsburgh. But when I explained where it had really come from, and how accidentally I had come across it, the heart-shaped river rock took on a whole new meaning to them. Without my saying so, Megan and Huck knew the one-of-a-kind remembrance of their wedding day carried extra special blessings for them. The angel bumps that emerged all over them told them so. From my perspective, the new-found heartifact represented a heavenly toast to the newlyweds. Neil clearly agreed with what I had concluded just prior to the wedding: where Megan is concerned, mere words are inadequate.

TWELVE

MY FATHER'S HEART

My finding solace from grief through heart stones completely underwhelmed my father for quite some time. He was living with his own grief during the same period, and he could hardly believe I was *still* speaking publicly about heart rocks six years after the first one appeared. My father had several concerns, including the fragility of the downtrodden parents I had been addressing (as if I was not one of them myself). While I understood his standoffish attitude, I also reminded him that the call I was answering had not originated within my own mind; my story had been solicited. I simply provided it with sincerity.

Another consideration with which my dad wrestled was the incomprehensible gravity of my loss. He could not imagine how a heart-shaped *anything* could carry such profound meaning for me in the wake of my son's death. In retrospect, I think my father perceived heartifacts as dangerous decoys that prevented me from coping with grief properly and could potentially lead me away from reality altogether. I have to admit, the whole phenomenon was peculiar, and it made me question a lot of things. I still marvel that anything could dampen the monstrous pain of my grieving for Neil the way my first heartifact did. That one alone allowed me to reconnect with hope. And hope was something I desperately needed by the time it found me.

To reiterate, when Neil died, my father and I were already six months into grieving the cancer death of our Evelyn. Coping with the loss of two people so central to our happiness was complicated for each of us. As I have already intimated, my father and I handled our grief very differently. Fortunately, we recognized this. Back in 2007, when my father bellowed, "Face it, Margaret, death is death," I believe he was *sincerely* concerned for me. He knew I was recovering from multiple losses, navigating through severe grief, when he took issue with my story about heartifacts.

While my mind understood my father's analysis about the finality of death, my heart simply could not embrace his conclusion. Besides my own struggles, I had to help Neil's siblings make sense of their losses, too. Their world had literally imploded, and their trust in most things had been shattered. Besides the obvious losses each of my surviving children had suffered since 1998, I imagine they also feared that Neil's fate could also befall them. Why wouldn't they?

Thankfully, we did have heartifacts; at the very least, they met my children's emergent lack of trust and wounded faith halfway. From my point of view, heaven had provided the beacons of hope and healing for all of us. Whether or not it made sense to anyone else, simple, natural heart stones quelled my grieving family's anxieties like nothing else had. Then, when they started showing up by the dozens, we knew we were not too far adrift. Our heart stones were spiritual pay dirt…and they were more than coincidental.

With all due respect to my grieving father, my mother Evelyn's passing—while sad and difficult—was in synchrony with the natural cycle of life. She had lived eighty-one very full years, her marriage had stood the test of time, and she had been blessed with the loving support of her eleven children. Conversely, watching a child's life pass before your own makes no sense to a parent. It is out of order, and it is no small thing to sustain a grieving parent through the remainder of his or her natural life. This is precisely why I believe God took a unique approach when comforting me, even if my father could not relate.

My dad and I grieved differently. That's all. And we lovingly gave each other wide berths for our individual styles. I accepted his parental admonishment for my outside-the-box approach to grieving; but privately, I dismissed it every time I gazed upon my garden full of heart rocks. My dad and I never formally discussed the elephants in the room—his grief and mine. We did not need to. Instead, we respected each other and carried on. In our hearts, each of us knew how much the other one hurt, and we accepted that neither of us could prescribe a remedy to the other.

Simply put, there are many ways to grieve, and none is "best." Grief is as unique as a fingerprint.

Years later, my father made a surprising discovery that altered his perception of my crazy heart stones. I learned this when I received an unusually enthusiastic call from my sister, Maureen, in April of 2007. During the previous year, she had moved into our family home to care for our aging father. At first, Maureen was Dad's proverbial "right arm." As time passed, however, she became his left arm, legs, eyes, and ears. (The one thing our father never needed support with was his mind. Intellectually, he never missed a beat.)

When I received Maureen's call from 1108 Greentree Road, I had been preparing for another memorial service talk at Children's Hospital. She had placed the phone call at Dad's behest. He wanted me to come over as quickly as possible.

"Is everything all right, Maureen?" I asked.

She confirmed that all was well, but added, "Dad needs to see you."

I found this to be a little surprising. I shut down my laptop and told Maureen I would be right over.

But before we hung up, Maureen shared one more thing: "He has a gift for you."

Now I was even more curious (and excited)! As one of eleven children, gifting was most often done en masse. You can only imagine how unusual it was to be singled out.

I got going.

When I arrived at 1108, Maureen made sure to greet me first. She felt I needed a little background before I saw Dad. It would explain the significance of the gift I was about to receive.

She began, "It seems Dad was reminiscing about Mom again today, this time while sifting through trinkets in her jewelry box." I knew what that meant. It had been a tender, sentimental day for Jim Horgan.

"During the process, Dad was shocked to find something he had long forgotten. That is when he called out to me with the strangest urgency in his voice," she said.

I was all ears.

Maureen continued. "When I got to Mom and Dad's room, he extended his opened hands toward me, one cupping the other. There, in the middle of his top hand, was a small, heart-shaped bit of seashell.

"That is when he pronounced, 'This must be for Maggie!'"

Dad then provided a history of the little blush-colored heart to Maureen. He told her he had discovered it on a beach in New Guinea while stationed there during World War II. After finding it the first time, he refined and polished the fragment before sending the love token to our mother who was back home. On the day my father showed the memory-laden heart from the South Pacific to Maureen, at least seventy years had passed. He had no idea that Mom had saved the tiny shell. It stunned Dad to find that special heart, safe and sound. It had been in the room he and my mother shared for decades!

As the Second World War had expanded to include the United States, James Francis Horgan heard Uncle Sam's call to duty. He answered by enlisting in the Navy in 1942. It was not an easy choice for a young man in love to make; he was head over heels with the hometown girl who would later become his wife and our mother. The two were like many other young American couples who shared a similar challenge during the 1940s. Jim became a Seabee and was deployed to New Hebrides for the duration. Evelyn Louise Murray, my mother, awaited Jim's return in Duquesne, Pennsylvania. During the war, she was an office worker at The United States Steel Corporation's Duquesne Works. My parents married each other on December 29, 1943, during the sailor's Christmas leave.

Image 19. Evelyn L. Murray & James F. Horgan (1943)

After showing Maureen the heart from New Hebrides, our dad announced to her that he wanted to transform a small brass pillbox (which he also found among my mother's jewels) into a worthy home for the precious relic. He wanted to present the heart shell to me in regal fashion. Maureen promptly gathered the supplies my Seabee dad had requested: fabric (preferably velvet), gemstone embellishments, and a hot glue gun.

My aging father's intention was so endearing. Suddenly, the ninety-year-old needed to enshrine a heart shell he had not thought about since 1943! Its value had multiplied immeasurably since his Evelyn's passing. He was touched at how she had preserved it, albeit loosely, among other things she most treasured: the first lost teeth of her children, locks of her babies' first curls, and the hospital bracelets of those newborns. Rediscovering his own historic heartifact suddenly validated the ones I had been telling him about for seven years.

By finding his New Hebrides heart among the rest of my mother's jewels, my dad was shown how important the gift had been to my mother. His decision to give it to me confirmed something he could not previously embrace; he was now privy to the divine connection the living and deceased can continue to share. He could also grasp why my own heartifacts were precious to me.

My formerly skeptical father was preparing to tell me, "I get it, Maggie!"

Before I reached my father, Maureen made certain that I fully understood all of these details. I understood, and I appreciated. Unwittingly, Jim Horgan had embraced the power of a heartifact long before the term (or I) had ever been conceived!

Three-quarters of a century later, the heartifact he had once sent halfway around the globe was still creating magic. The heart-shaped seashell that had once lifted Evelyn's wanting spirit was now able to stir Jim's. The sincere love he had given freely in his youth found its way back to him in his old age. It was love as timeless and everlasting as he had first intended.

When my dad presented his precious find to me, he beamed with pride. I, in turn, huddled close to him in appreciation. I never felt as connected to both my parents as I did right then. What multiplied the value of his gift, beyond measure, was the heavenly connection we both felt with our beloved ones, Evelyn and Neil. Neither space nor time nor death could suppress the message symbolized by heartifacts showing up so perfectly in both of our lives.

**Image 20. My father, James Horgan, 90, with his 1943 heartifact,
the Heart of New Hebrides (2008)**

I hardly knew how to thank my dad for giving me such a personal and profound gift. His grief over my mother's death was fresh and painful for him every day he lived on in her absence. I also had God to thank for being so endlessly present in my life. In appreciation, I give to Him all that I am: my joys, my sorrows, my laughter, and my tears. To my father, an Irishman and a poet, I gave the following in appreciation for the cherished heart:

THE HEART OF NEW HEBRIDES

One young man, so far from home,
Was tanned in the South Pacific.
An Irishman, from steel town shores,
He must have looked *terrific*!

Strapping and lean, with dark and dense curls,
Though closely cropped—I'm sure,
This man becomes "Dad" in a few more years,
For his love for my mother was pure.

She was a princess—a queen in the making;
As such, she held on for her king.
The young couple's kingdom? It spanned the globe!
Their love was a wonderful thing.

But the distance, it did leave a pang in his chest,
In spite of the work to be done.
He built air strips and huts, so the homeland could rest,
While missing the sight of his "one."

On a day that afforded some musing,
Young Jim spied a shell on the beach.
It was polished and painted by Nature herself,
And the shape he sought was within reach.

There were plenty of tools at the ready,
But Jim's vision required the best.
With the keenest and sharpest knife of the bunch,
He notched what he would send to the nest.

The size of the gift? It was modest;
Barely more than that of a dime.
Jim refined the heart he envisioned,
For the girl he would marry in time.

Well, marry they did (the next winter).
And the seasons have come and have gone.
Now the queen, who cherished the treasure,
Waits in peace, as her king trudges on.

Jim is weary and sad for he misses Ev so,
As he studies the jewels left behind.
How could life, which held such promise back then,
Turn out to be so unkind?

She knows Jim is aching, but doing his work
At completing what they had begun.
The eleven children, the branches they grew,
Will continue as though they were one.

But a daughter, Ev fears, needs to hear from her mom
(One who lost a boy...barely a man).
With hearts that keep her son's spirit alive,
Maggie copes in the best way she can.

So the shell the king finds among all the jewels,
Leaves him no other choice but to sing;
"This gift of a heart, I sent over the sea,
To my youngest girl, I must bring!"

Then his queen declared, in her most demure way,
(The way she embraced all her life),
"The heart sent to me is for Maggie now.
All the hearts, they are saving her life.

Our Neil now joins our tradition, Jim;
Sharing hearts…to calm longing tears.
Maggie's boy, no, *her angel*, knows just what to do;
He sends hearts to erase all her fears."

Since receiving the one and only poem I have ever written, my father has joined his queen, his Evelyn.

My parents were special people who had faith in God and in each other. My father was a lover of life, a scholar, an athlete, a wit, a poet, and a true family man. Words seem inadequate when describing my mother, Evelyn Murray Horgan. She was just so lovely…and so good.

God gave me outstanding parents, amazing siblings, and the courage to build a family of my own. My children and I consider ourselves fortunate to be extensions of Jim and Evelyn's love.

THIRTEEN

A PREORDAINED LIFE?

Tapping into the Horgan family tree could inspire a very, very long book of its own, but that is not my purpose. What is relevant to *Heartifacts* is an understanding of Neil's impact on my family and his father's. Neil loved them both and was an understated but profound member of each. His death left its mark on dozens of cousins, aunts, and uncles and his absence created a void that still reverberates through the generations. We do our best to fill it with beautiful, cherished memories of our Neil.

Thankfully, Neil passed from this life peacefully; he had no regrets and left no one worse off for having known him. I think the members of both his families would agree: Neil swept through our lives like a gentle breeze and helped all of us shine a little more brightly.

Image 21. Neil (center, with hat on backward) among Horgan cousins at Grandma & Pop Pop's (Green Tree, PA, 1997)

As you can see, Horgans are no strangers to babies. From the time Neil was born, he was surrounded! Even so, something about him stood out. When he was less than a year old, one of my sisters-in-law (who had just had her fifth child) even teased me about how perfect Neil was. I just shrugged my shoulders and accepted the compliment on Neil's behalf. I had not done anything to make Neil be anything other than who he already was. From my perspective, Neil had been born reasonable and easy to love.

I always felt in sync with Neil, but I think many other people felt a similar peace while in his company. Much like the effortless flowing of his circulation, there seemed to be an inherent soundness and grace that coursed through him. For me, it begs the following questions: What made Neil so easy to be around? What was it that made him so impactful, even before cancer drew so much attention to him?

Recently, my sister Joyce gave a gift to me that may have shed light on the answers to those questions. After unwrapping the present, I was surprised to find a thirty-one-year-old photograph of Neil and me, ensconced in a brand-new, personalized picture frame. It was engraved with my own words, a quote from the manuscript for this book: "The heart stones were surely not random. They were meant precisely for me and presented at a time when I most needed them...Gifts from the indomitable spirit of my son, Neil."

I immediately remembered the day the picture had been taken. I also recalled having seen the photograph before. But seeing those words engraved beneath the print made me consider my life with Neil in its entirety. The 1982 snapshot shows my eleven-month-old reaching for something in the waters of Mingo Creek, while I am seated on a rock right behind him; I am holding onto my little explorer by the back of his overalls.

Joyce, who had originally captured the scene on film all those years ago, saw the old photo in a whole new light more recently.

In her own words, she remarked, "When I found this picture of you and Neil among my photo albums this year, I couldn't help but wonder if he was reaching for a heart rock!"

I could see her point: Neil was definitely going for something in the water. What struck me most, however, was neither Neil nor me; it was the large reflection of light on the surface of the water above my son. The illuminated area, which took up about a third of the photograph, was heart-shaped! Seeing this for the first time after so many years shocked me; I had had a copy of the same photo in one of my own family albums for over three decades! I also found it astounding that the point at the base of the heart was aimed directly at little Neil.

**Image 22. Maggie, 24 & Neil, 11 mos., at Mingo
Creek State Park (Pennsylvania, 1982)**

Joyce gave this gift to me in a room filled with other family members. They all admired it, but it took each of them a moment to see what had just jumped out at my heart-trained eyes. The heart shining on the water upstream from Neil was now *so* obvious to me; I could hardly believe I had never noticed it before! As the newly framed photograph was passed from person to person, expressions like "Ooh!" and "Aah!" and "No way!" dotted the room. Each exclamatory remark acknowledged that he or she had seen the heart of light in the resurrected picture. Once it became apparent to everyone, those undeniable goose bumps (a.k.a. angel bumps) were all over each of us simultaneously! Had Neil been leading us to hearts all along? The new revelation in the old picture was so unexpected and innocent—we could not help but wonder.

In truth, the photograph had not changed; our vision had. And that is exactly what happened to my perception of death and experience with grief when my first heartifact appeared. On that day, I had been guided away from the most painful, hopeless emotions I had ever felt. Through a heart stone, I received a spiritual awakening that God knew I needed. He did, indeed, deliver me to a better place with tangible tokens of love and compassion. Fortunately, the phenomenal experience continues. When I least expect it, another heart stone leads me further along.

FOURTEEN

FULL CIRCLE

During the process of writing this book, I never anticipated how I might draw it to a close. I have so many anecdotal stories about heart rocks finding me since 2001; I could go on and on! In retrospect, I should have known that a perfect heart rock would bring the story full circle at precisely the right time.

Last fall, in 2012, a picture-perfect Indian summer day prompted my son Davin and me to escape suburbia and head for the hills. It was also a perfect opportunity to include our family dogs, Lucky and Tank. Naturally, we ended up at our favorite mountain spot near Ligonier, Pennsylvania: Linn Run, the creek where we found Neil's twenty-first birthday heartifact eleven years earlier. Davin, a landlubber, was happy to keep our cell phones and camera dry by hiking along the trail beside the stream. I, on the other hand, could not stay out of the water! Thanks to the treacherously slick, moss-covered rocks scattered about the creek bottom, even the dogs would not embrace the challenge with me. That day, I found myself hiking solo through the crystal-clear mountain brook.

Before too long, I discovered a sturdy walking stick atop some of the larger rocks in the creek. I concluded that the four-foot-long support, with a two-inch diameter, was so perfect that it had probably accompanied a previous hiker. That kind soul must have known the next explorer could use it, too. I knew such a stick could make the difference in my trek being manageable or not, so I decided to borrow it. The discarded tree branch, worn smooth, became indispensable to me as I headed downstream toward Flatrock. The natural landmark, where Linn Run's creek bed emerges as a single, massive, slippery rock, is well-known to locals but not to weekenders. Flatrock is sheltered by forest and takes up the width of the stream—about thirty to forty feet. The formation is equal in length. While growing up, my siblings and I considered Flatrock one of our family's best-kept secrets.

No one knows how long Flatrock has been reputed as the nature-made Slip 'N Slide it still is. Its slick surface has always made it nearly impossible to walk upon, but so much fun to slide down. Flatrock enthusiasts know the best methods for doing so involve using practically any surface of the body *except* the bottoms of your feet: your belly, your bottom, your shins—it's your choice! With such a destination as my goal, creek-hiking to the watery fun spot made me feel like a kid again.

In the past, I had been the little sister who never seemed to catch up with her Huck Finn-like brothers, especially when we all ventured through the same creek toward the same spot. Besides, "the boys" (seven of them) were always capturing mini lobster-looking creatures from beneath the rocks. This activity usually kept me at a distance. The indigenous freshwater crustaceans I describe are called crayfish. I might have been a young naturalist, but only to a point; I steered clear of anything that bit or pinched. In 2012, however, I was determined to finally tackle the Linn Run challenge.

Before going any further, I have a random confession to announce: I have become a bit sensitive about this whole heartifact phenomenon in recent years. I know plenty of people who think *maybe* it has become an obsession, or *maybe* I should just get past grief...even if it is good grief. They don't have to say a word; my antennae are up! By now, I am as attuned to my critics as I am to noticing heart rocks. Respectfully, I accept their skepticism but am not dissuaded by it. The heart stones that have trickled into my life have helped me to manage my grief. *That is a fact.* Whether or not it appeals to everyone, *heart rocks do indeed find me.*

Due to the personal sensitivity I have just described, while hiking the creek most recently I very deliberately announced to Davin, "I am not hiking through the stream in search of heart rocks, you know; I am just proving to myself that I can make it all the way to Flatrock. I have no plans to retreat to the trail like I used to."

Davin just nodded and waved in my direction, probably knowing a heart rock would find me despite my own intentions. They always do!

Davin, the dogs, and I remained within earshot of one another during my forty-minute downstream adventure. I found my water hike exhilarating and full of rarities. Along the way, I even saw a native rainbow trout swim around one of my ankles! I had never imagined that anything but skittish crayfish inhabited the shallow stream.

Shortly after that, I lost my footing, slid into the water, and got soaked. Of course I did! I had been pressing my luck all along. Falling in was usually just a matter of time in Linn Run; the slippery rocks usually lived up to their reputations. I didn't much mind submitting to the water, but its temperature above my ankles was shocking. Cold is no friend to my body, either. Knowing I could not remain in wet clothes for too long, I picked up my pace as I headed around the last bend in the stream on my way to meeting Davin, Lucky, and Tank.

While still trudging my waterlogged self toward Flatrock, I noticed my trailblazers were at the edge of the creek beside me. When Davin saw me (grinning from ear to ear and up to my waist in water), he smiled, dipped his gaze toward the ground, and shook his head from side to side. That is when we both laughed at my condition.

In order to redeem myself, I triumphantly called out to him, "I made it, Dav!"

Then I announced, "I'll be right there," and proceeded toward a reasonable exit point at the bank of the creek.

Taking each of my steps judiciously, I was attentive to where I placed my walking stick and feet. During this process I spotted something in my path that I could not ignore. By now, you have probably already guessed what it was.

Yes, there in the water was another heart rock! This one was stunning. It was not huge, but it surely was shaped like a heart. The rugged markings on it seemed to tell a story; but when I picked up the new specimen, I was a little surprised to find that it was very smooth. The unique stone had that extra special quality, too: it felt good in the hands…soothing and substantial, but not heavy.

"Is this rock another too-good-to-pass-up heartifact?" I wondered.

I tossed the newfound heart stone onto Flatrock and asked my second son what he thought. "Do I need this one, Davin? Or has this heartifact thing gone too far?"

He replied, "I don't know, Mom, but it's a good heart-shaped rock! Maybe having one more won't hurt."

Image 23. Another Linn Run heartifact (Adam's Falls, PA, September 2012)

I agreed, shrugged my shoulders, and put the newly christened heartifact into my Windbreaker pocket. Then the four of us hustled back to the car along the trail, another enchanting byway. No longer needing it, I leaned the walking stick against a towering pine tree. Another hiker would be as delighted to find it as I had been at the outset of my momentous journey to Flatrock. Davin and I then forged on toward where we had parked, along with our canine companions.

When we arrived at the car, I was happy to discover my gym bag contained shoes and a change of clothes. I hastily donned my dry togs. Even so, my core remained chilled from the brisk water of the stream. Seeking relief, Davin, the dogs, and I hopped into the car and then headed to the nearest town. Visiting the historic village of Ligonier, about twelve miles away, often punctuated a memorable day in the mountains for us. Besides, I could hardly wait to get to a steaming cup of hot coffee.

Fortunately, Abigail's Coffee Shop was still open when we arrived at the town square, but not for long. It was nearly closing time for all of the businesses dotting the square's perimeter. I parked the car at the next available spot and we headed inside. Along the way, we absorbed the ambiance of the quaint town. When we approached the shop's entrance, I noticed a single flyer displayed on its window. The bulletin was posted to encourage monetary donations for a local seventeen-year-old who was fighting Ewing's sarcoma. This teenager had the very same cancer that had killed Neil! I was taken aback; it's just not every day that I hear of a child with the devastating diagnosis that hits too close to home. It rattled me to be reminded of it, especially when Davin and I were having such a perfectly restorative and playful day otherwise.

After entering Abigail's, I asked the two teenagers who were brewing coffee if they knew anything about the local teen fighting Ewing's. Both baristas were perplexed by my question and had no idea what I was talking about. Since business was light, they stepped outside to read the petition I had described. Neither of them knew the afflicted boy.

Feeling I owed the young coffee crafters an explanation, I expressed why the flyer had piqued my interest. I shared my losing Neil to the very same pediatric bone cancer the Ligonier boy was fighting. I also expressed that the young man was engaged in a very difficult battle. It was then that one of the workers, Ben, admitted knowing more about Ewing's sarcoma than any teen wants to; he had lost a close family friend to the disease only seven months earlier. The victim who Ben knew personally was only eleven years old when Ewing's was discovered in her pelvis. Within eight months, the unrelenting disease had taken the young girl's life. I could hardly believe what I was hearing—again!

What was this *supposedly* rare cancer doing to the kids of this unsuspecting little mountain town? It was all so disturbing. My memory was jarred and could not help but gallop back in time. Standing before Ben, digesting all that I had just learned while simply trying to get a cup of coffee, I silently remembered Neil's hospital roommate in 1999. Jimmy, who also fought bone cancer, had been from the area, too.

Silenced, Davin and I stepped outside with our hot espresso drinks and sat at one of the café tables in front of Abigail's. It seemed our search for the comforting beverages walked us right back into our own family's nightmare. The high spirits we had arrived with became weighed down with concern for the seventeen-year-old confronting cancer and sadness for the family who had lost their little girl just as we had lost Neil.

I couldn't help but want to do something. A donation for the boy could be arranged, but what about the grieving family? I asked myself.

Then I decided—I could remember her.

With that on my mind, I stepped back into the café and asked Ben if he would express my sympathies to his young friend's family. "Could you please tell them, another parent who understands their loss will always remember their little girl?"

Ben agreed to pass my sympathies along.

Then, I admitted to him, "It would be easier for me to keep my promise if I knew her name.

"A first name will suffice," I added.

Without hesitation, Ben replied, "Her name was Maggie."

"Wow, her name is Maggie," I quietly murmured to myself, while my knees buckled slightly.

I looked directly at Ben and said, "How ironic—my name is Maggie, too!"

Now, Maggie is not that common a name. The coincidence caused the hair on my arms to stand up immediately. When that happens, I know I have made a connection to something special, maybe even something supernatural. The affirmation assured me I was on the right path with Ben and little Maggie. My intuition never fails me when I get such feedback.

I followed by asking Ben if he would assure little Maggie's grieving family of one thing: "This Maggie will *never* forget their Maggie."

It is natural for grieving parents, like me, to entertain fears that their beloved, deceased child will be forgotten. I thought my pledge to them might bring a little comfort in this regard. Even if I was a total stranger, at least I was a relevant one.

I returned to Davin, who had remained at a table outside the shop. When I told him the little girl who died from Ewing's was named Maggie, he and I *both* got the chills! By now, my mind was processing all that was unfolding that afternoon. I found it difficult to settle in. Enjoying the hot beverage I had driven an extra twenty minutes for was no longer my focus. Then, it struck me.

"Davin, you know the new heart rock I found at Flatrock today? It must be for Maggie's family!"

Without delay, Davin headed toward our car, retrieved the stone from under the driver's seat, and brought the newest heartifact back to me. At my request, he had also grabbed one of my business cards from the car. I needed something on which to jot a note to accompany the heart rock. Since I work for a familiar Western Pennsylvania company, and my cards have my picture on them, I hoped using one would help legitimize my intentions for Maggie's family. My condolences and my promise were sincere.

Ben had come across as thoughtful and compassionate during our two brief conversations. Based upon the demeanor of my brand-new acquaintance, I felt he might not mind delivering both the heart stone and my note to his grieving family friends. Fortunately, my assessment of Ben was accurate. After a brief explanation about the heart stone, and why I wanted to pass it along, Ben carefully and respectfully accepted my offering. He then promised to deliver the meaning-filled heart to Maggie's family.

Although I wasn't sure how the grieving family would take to the mysterious gift, I was sure heaven had placed the perfect messenger in my path. Ben would carry out the mission. Yes, through him, little Maggie's heart would find its way home. I felt certain her family would "get it."

A few days later, I heard a new voice on my cell phone upon reviewing messages from calls I had missed. When I realized the unfamiliar voice was that of Maggie's mother, I listened attentively, even somewhat anxiously. She identified herself as Cyndi.

I had hoped I would hear from someone in Maggie's family, especially if they had a positive reaction to what I had given to them. By using my business card as a note card, I had provided them with my cell phone number. Cyndi's message revealed that she was comfortable with my modest memorial to her daughter, Maggie. Only then did I feel assured that I had not overstepped any delicate lines.

In a gentle and sincere voice, Cyndi expressed being grateful that I had reached out to her family. She clearly appreciated the heart rock I had sent her way, along with my intentions for her family's healing. Thankfully, I had not made an enormous mistake. At one point during her message, Cyndi even giggled softly at the notion of her Maggie and my Neil collaborating in order to bring the two of us together with a heart rock. What a comforting, even happy, notion from someone who could have justifiably been embittered over her loss.

When Cyndi concluded her message with, "I love the heart rock," I felt very happy that I had followed my instincts at Abigail's Coffee Shop. On that note especially, I looked forward to returning her call at the next appropriate opportunity.

The perfect time to do so came a few days later. But, I have to admit, I still had to psych myself into actually dialing her number. In preparation for the call I reminded myself that the Linn Run heart stone had already broken the ice for me. Truthfully, Maggie's mother and I had already connected! In the grand scheme of things, the phone calls were a simple formality. I trusted that the magic of the heartifact we shared would keep everybody safe.

Once I reached Cyndi by phone, we spoke as only two tender mothers yearning to make sense of life could. Both of us had been entrusted with loving and beautiful children who, without warning, had become medically fragile and died. Nothing in life prepares a parent for that. But thanks to one obscure heart stone, we now had each other to share the journeys life had forced upon each of us. During our first phone conversation, we agreed a face-to-face meeting was something we both wanted to arrange.

Within two weeks of that call, I returned to Ligonier to meet Cyndi in person. We planned to have lunch together. When I first met her, two things captured my attention immediately: her blue eyes. They were as bright as crystals and as deep as the sea. I could plainly see that there was so much behind them.

As I stood there facing Cyndi (and despite what I had been through myself), my mind silently questioned, "How could life be so cruel and eyes so telling?"

In that moment, I even wondered if my own eyes had appeared as betrayed when my loss of Neil was as new as Cyndi's loss of little Maggie. I considered that there must still be times when certain people, sensitive people, can look into my eyes and see the agony they have witnessed all these years later. Perhaps all parents who have suffered the loss of a child have eyes that forever bear witness to the vacancy left behind.

After registering the vulnerability I detected in Cyndi's eyes, I could hardly believe I had made it through my first year of grieving for Neil, let alone eleven of them. How I wished I could erase her pain, but that is beyond anyone's abilities; even time cannot do that completely. That must be where heaven steps in.

Yes, thank heaven for small miracles, I reminded myself. Thank heaven for heartifacts! Cyndi and I, still strangers, politely hugged each other's pain and silently recognized each other's irreplaceable loss. Then we headed through a misty rain to share our meal at a local grill.

Once seated at the casual eatery, Cyndi and I glided into conversation rather quickly, but carefully, too. Our exchange flowed naturally. I doubt anyone in the crowded restaurant could have guessed that we had just met.

"How long can each of us hold it together while sharing our stories in this busy place?" I silently asked myself, as we paused to look over our menus.

Well, Cyndi and I did manage to remain composed throughout the meal. At one point, we acknowledged that our coming together seemed destined to happen by virtue of little Maggie, Neil, and the heart rock relay a few weeks earlier. Cyndi and I were very glad to have met. We had simply followed our hearts.

During lunch, we shared a lot of thoughts that would probably have been unnatural to discuss with anyone who had not lost a child. Obviously, the things we knew we had in common were devastating: each of us witnessing our own child's confrontation with cancer, each of us keeping a pulse on the impact of such a loss on our surviving children, and, in the end, each of us having to prepare our child to transition from this life. We discussed God and many unanswerable questions. We both agreed, ours was a new normal—a normal either of us would have gladly declined, given the choice.

Without even realizing it, Cyndi and I talked until all the other patrons had left the restaurant. By default, we figured each of us should head back to our respective homes, too. As we wrapped up our afternoon, Cyndi and I still marveled at how a heart rock had initiated the chain of events that ultimately brought us together.

"Another heartifact to the rescue!" I silently celebrated.

Then, almost as an afterthought, Cyndi added, "Oh, did I tell you—I knew about you and your heart stones long before receiving the one you had asked Ben to deliver to me."

I was puzzled. "How could that be?" I asked her.

Her explanation was bittersweet. "Just before we left Children's Hospital to bring Maggie home for hospice care, a nurse pulled me aside and told me about your finding heart stones since shortly after your son's death. I guess she was trying to give me something hopeful to reflect upon as I prepared myself for life without Maggie. The nurse, Carol May, told me how you thought heaven made it possible for Neil to connect with you after his passing. I left the hospital wondering if my little Maggie would also find a way to reach me from the other side of life. I could only hope that what the compassionate nurse reported about you and your son could be true for me and Maggie, too."

I was stunned that a medical professional believed my story could help not only grieving parents, but also a parent facing the incomprehensible task of supporting her eleven-year-old daughter as she approached death. This new information made *every* risk of my being misunderstood (or categorized as someone who just couldn't "move on") worth it. No, mine is not a mission I would have ever dreamed up for myself, but it is one I have been willing to accept on behalf of all of us who grieve for our children.

On the day I met little Maggie's mother, I was astounded to learn that the impact of heartifacts had already been so far-reaching. The healing message of the heart stones had truly gone full circle. In fact, it was budding into a legend on its own merit. Accepting this truth gave me the resolve I needed to stop equivocating and *finish the book*.

The advice Neil inspired years ago, when I prepared to present my first speech to grieving parents, came to the forefront of my mind all over again. "Just Do It," I reminded myself. This time, however, I imagined little Maggie chiming in!

Even during my most recent conversation with her, Cyndi specifically urged me to, "Press on!"

I promised her I would, and added, "I think your Maggie will help see me through to the book's conclusion."

In appreciation, I dedicate this chapter to Maggie, along with her friend Ben, and my trooper, Davin. They were all pivotal in relaying the heartifact that brought Cyndi a degree of hope and *Heartifacts* to this astounding crossroad.

**Image 24. Maggie Horgan & Cyndi McGinnis
with first heartifacts (November 2012)**

The events captured in this chapter reinforce what I have been trying to communicate throughout this book and demystify how divine communication can work. To her mother and me, the journey of little Maggie's heart rock also reinforces some powerful and reassuring spiritual truths:

True love is forever.
God is attentive.
Heaven is interactive.
We, on Earth, have divine helpers.

By now, I hope it is obvious that *Heartifacts* goes way beyond my own thoughts and impressions. I bring it to you as an inspired work that I cannot help but share. When my tears of grief joined the Pacific

Ocean, the grace of God delivered a heart stone to me. At the same moment, my son's spirit wrapped itself around me in a way I never thought possible. Then the sun setting, the moon illuminating, the tides shifting, and Mother Earth creating, collaborated with heaven and magnified the message with heartifacts two and three.

Yes, the heavenly support I had wished and prayed for filled my hands with symbols of love that were impossible to ignore. I immediately knew that they represented indestructible, compassionate, persistent, and immutable love.

I have taken a leap of faith by bringing *Heartifacts* to you, for there is nothing I can prove. But that is exactly what I did when I made my first speech and also when I handed a heart rock found in a mountain stream to a coffee barista in the little mountain town of Ligonier, Pennsylvania. One thing is certain: to some of us, a heart can make all the difference.

FIFTEEN

THE CHERRY ON TOP

On December 25, 2012, Gregory joined Lauren and some of her fellow ski instructors in Telluride, Colorado. They were all on the slopes celebrating the Christmas holiday together. My two skiers had a blast, but they could not help having the balance of our family on their minds during the sentimental holiday. Lauren and Greg missed Neil particularly, especially since he had inspired their love of skiing in the first place. They knew Neil would have devoured a skiing expedition in Telluride.

Just for fun, Dan, a member of their entourage, mounted a GoPro camera on his ski helmet. He had programmed it to take a photo every ten minutes throughout the day. The candidness of images captured in this manner makes viewing them for the first time like opening a wrapped gift. You never know what you will get.

When they finished skiing, Dan flipped through the digital thumbnail images that the automatic camera had taken. Meanwhile, Lauren looked at the same pictures from over his shoulder. Her eyes picked up on something Dan's had not. She then asked him if she could have a closer look at the snapshots of their day. Her eyes had not deceived her. Just as she thought, the picture of Greg completing his last ski run of the day included a heart-shaped cloud hanging in the sky above him! It appeared on the last photo the camera had taken that day.

Incredible!

Lauren was astounded! She then showed Greg, Dan, and the others. Lauren and Greg both knew the heart in the sky was no accident. They had been given a very special Christmas gift—a yuletide heartifact!

In no time, I received a text message from Lauren that included the extraordinary image. Davin and I reviewed the picture before reading Lauren's text, and we knew exactly why she had sent it. When we finally did read Lauren's caption describing the scene, we felt our Christmas was complete, too.

Her text message read, "A pic taken of Greg while we were skiing today. Looks like somebody came along for the powder…"

Image 25. The cherry on top, a candid snapshot of heart
cloud over Greg (Telluride, CO, Christmas 2012)

SIXTEEN

ALL MY HEARTS

*W*ell, there it is, Neil—the legend I call Heartifacts. Ours continues to be a journey I could have never imagined. Perhaps I had to write it to believe it. If nothing more, I hope these chapters are a testament to remarkable love—love that heals and protects. Being your mother has blessed and enriched me. I am ever grateful that God ever gave me the privilege. Hard as it was to lose you, it was far better than not having had you in my life at all. I am flooded with memories as I try to close. Recording events that unfolded and became your life has been surreal. I would like to share just one more.

When you came home from Penn State for Thanksgiving break in November of 2000, I knew you would not be returning to school the minute I saw you. There was no color left in your face—pain had stolen it. Making it only halfway up the steps from the foyer, you leaned against the wall, looked up at me and said, "I should have come home weeks ago, Mom...I missed you so much."

All I could say in return was, "Oh, Neil."

You never mentioned how sick you were leading up to Thanksgiving, or how much pain you had been in during the four-hour drive home. But later, your friend Sarah did.

She tearfully elaborated, "Neil was in so much pain during the drive home; it forced him to pull his Jeep off the road several times. It was so frightening and sad. He could hardly even shift gears."

Poor Sarah felt helpless as Neil struggled to get them home. "If I had only known how to drive a stick shift," she lamented.

It did not surprise me that you completed the trip home in spite of your pain, Neil. You were not a quitter.

I can also guess at why you did not come home sooner. For one, you knew the hideous drill that awaited you, if cancer had returned. Secondly, you stayed on at PSU to squeeze every drop you could out of the college life you had earned. Being there was one of your dreams come true. When our eyes met on the stairway, all I could do was admire your tenacity and innocence. To be present for you took every-thing in me at that moment. Inside myself, I wailed in silence from the pit of my being. When we finally embraced, there on the steps, we both knew we were not alone. Cancer had pierced our hearts again. Your returning to the hospital was inevitable.

The very next day you were admitted to Children's for more prob-ing and testing. Like déjà vu, we ingested the familiar medical agen-da presented to you. The first order of business was another total body scan. You agreed to the exam, and I escorted you (along with my rosary beads).

Not a thing about the room we entered had changed. It was as sterile and barren as it had been sixteen months earlier—when you were first diagnosed. While someone prepared you for the Magnetic Resonance Imaging (MRI), I sat alone in a chair against one of the walls— feeling like worry might swallow me whole. The likely outcome of the test loomed large as the kind stranger left the room.

Then, the voice of a technician who we could not see spoke to us. Her words echoed within the clinical chamber as if they had originated in deep space. You and I were attentive and followed instructions to perfection, as if our obedience could buy your escape from Ewing's sarcoma. I watched and I prayed as you listened (and, no doubt, prayed). Then you and the table you were on were fed into the massive tube of the MRI machine. As instructed, you remained motionless while the notorious clicking and banging of the imaging procedure commenced. The haunting sounds of the machine took turns chirping, like the voices of aliens discussing your fate. The MRI results would be conclusive. Your future hung in the balance.

While the scanning took place, I sat in the twilight of that room as bravely as I could. Silent tears streamed down my face for the duration, but I hoped you would never notice. Just imagining what was running through your nineteen-year-old mind while you were inside that cold and dimly lit hollow made me want to crawl out of my skin and into yours; I never wanted you to be alone in such frightening circumstances. I had to do something. So, I petitioned God.

My intellect fully appreciated why He would call one so sweet out of this difficult and often disappointing world, but my quaking heart pleaded otherwise. I even promised God that you would make a stellar survivor—given the chance. I pleaded your case to all of heaven. Upon reflection, I am sure I was pleading my own case, too. I begged, as any parent would, but my pleas would not change the outcome of the MRI. Waiting in that room, I experienced the most helpless feeling I have ever known.

The thought of losing you was incomprehensible, Neil. When you entered my world, so did a special elixir of joy, goodness, compassion, and gentle wisdom. Those attributes defined you and touched everyone who knew you. Demonstrating things like genuine interest in a person, patience, and unconditional love was as natural as breathing to you. Ever since you were little, you seemed to know that people shine brighter when they are surrounded by kindness. You provided kindness. Only a good and loving God would share a person like you with the rest of us, even if you could not stay for long. I believe He needs to give the world a sampling of heaven, every now and then.

The truth is, Mom, most grieving parents feel this way about their little saints and soldiers. That is why what all of you have gone through cuts so deeply and hurts so pervasively. What joined all of you, who are bereaved, to all of us who have died, was not exclusive to our human existence, though. All of us share a spirit that is not confined to the limits of the physical world; therefore, death has no power over us—unless we forget or turn away from that truth.

Given the smallest amount of sincere faith, even shredded and angry faith, the Spirit of God can sculpt miracles in human lives. Hearts are the conduit by which the Holy Spirit reaches us. That is why an inanimate stone, shaped like a heart, took on new meaning the minute you found your first in Carlsbad.

As I suggested in the beginning, Mom, "Keep it simple." Not-so-ordinary rocks became "heartifacts" because they represented our love for each other. Can you imagine what that stone went through to become a heart? A lot of hard knocks and surrender made it so. Perhaps even the most paralyzing grief can take on a new shape in time. The grieving are forever changed. "Business as usual" ceases to exist. Grief does not have to destroy a life, though. With the Holy Spirit, it can be folded into a new, broadened, and meaningful one.

I know it is not quite that simple, Mom. We have all been through a lot...you, me, my amigos...any family who grieves. Calling upon spiritual support is the secret to making sense of anything that truly matters. Death is unavoidable, but the rungs on heaven's ladder have a gentler pitch when supported by the Holy Spirit. Everyone will make the journey home, eventually.

In the meantime, choose a life that supports the love you are, Mom. That is my wish for you. It is everyone's birthright to live fully and happily. Just remember the equation: humans are much more than form and matter. They are timeless, limitless beings of spirit, too. Expressing your unique spirit can make all the difference in distinguishing a meaningful life from one to be endured. Just do it, Mom. I know you can!

Staying close to God will keep you strong. And when you are strong, Mom, my brothers and my sister will rise out of the confusion of their existence, too. Remember, their recovery has already begun, for they are not strangers to heartifacts. Reach toward the future with them, knowing the Holy Spirit will fill all of your sails. Relish each day, even the difficult ones. They are part of becoming who you were meant to be, too.

Yes, our physical parting was totally sad, but we were blessed through the process. Besides, children do not leave their loving families. That kind of love cannot be destroyed. Our hearts tell us so. That is exactly how I am still with you, and the reason you are so compelled to share your story...I mean "our" story.

Wow, Neil—all of this is blowing my mind! I mean it—I really need a minute. I have to catch my breath.

Hey, good job, Mom!

By the way, you "Just Did It!"

But, Neil, I'm a mess! And I am drenching the keyboard again.

That is okay, Mom. It comes with the territory.

Thank you for everything, Neil…especially the hearts. I love you so much…beyond words, really.

And *I love you*, Mom…

**Image 26. Neil's long-awaited first day of college at
Penn State University (August 19, 2000)**

with all my hearts!

Image 27. All my hearts (2014)

CONCLUDING REMARKS

Through *Heartifacts*, I hope I have shed fresh light on the all-encompassing presence of love—big love, God's love. It can carry us through any conceivable trial, even surviving a child. After my son's suffering and death, my own faith and hope were at an all-time low. When I found my first heart stone, after specifically pleading for divine direction, I knew my prayers were being heard. When I found two more within minutes, I felt my original conclusion being reinforced. To me, the occurrences were an expression of the Holy Spirit's boundless nature. The Spirit is a living one, available to support us through whatever challenges our human lives present.

All that has come to pass during my lifetime has prepared me to help others facing similar heartbreak. I have confronted grief and made peace with it, but I did not do it on my own. I believe the Holy Spirit's compassionate love fortified me in the presence of grief so heavy; it could have drowned me. The same divine love continues to connect me to my son, Neil, despite his passing in 2001. I feel certain our individual spirits can heal and connect with those we love, in any realm, with God.

Life does, indeed, go on.

Some things were never meant to be handled alone. The sooner our egos step aside and let God's Spirit merge with our own, the sooner we can heal from any of life's insults. When we engage our own spirit, and the messages available to us through it, doors can open for each of us in a miraculous way. I believe miracles are available to us every day. I also believe such miracles can bring us out of deep despair and dispense the grace necessary to guide us safely through our human experience...and beyond.

I hope my story of hearts exemplifies the transcendent nature of love, since we live in a world far more expansive and timeless than can be appreciated through our five rudimentary senses. When my broken-down life intersected with compassion from heaven and earth, I believe I witnessed a miracle. The miracle was the path of hearts and hope leading me out of the deepest sadness of my life. With God's guidance, Jesus' promise, the Holy Spirit's presence, my son's inspiration, and a heart broken *wide open,* I share what peace and acceptance I have found since his death. And it took more than a village; it took a universe.

INDEX OF IMAGES

INDEX OF IMAGES (continued)

TESTIMONIALS

I first heard Maggie Horgan's heartifact story in 2005 at our memorial service in remembrance of the children for whom we had cared. You could hear a pin drop as her story unfolded, and as the original heart stone made its way through the crowd, people held it as if it were a precious treasure. Since that time, I have heard Maggie's story numerous times. Each telling reveals something new for me, and the families who attend our memorial services always comment on the comfort they find in her sharing.

As a chaplain in a pediatric facility for ten years, I have come to appreciate that there is no greater pain than losing a child. Maggie does not deny or sugarcoat her experience of grief following Neil's death, which was compounded by so many other losses. A child represents the future, and losing a significant piece of the future causes a loss of hope many times. Her heartifacts story provides a ray of hope for all those experiencing a loss. The heart stones are proof that our relationships with those who have died continue – just in a different form.

Neil's story, especially the part about the heart stones, must be shared with those who are on the journey through grief. It provides a light for the darkest parts of the path. The hope it brings is amazing.

Sr. Lisa Balcerek, C.S.J.
Chaplain, Pastoral Care Department
Children's Hospital of Pittsburgh of UPMC
One Children's Hospital Drive
4401 Penn Avenue
Main Hospital - Sixth Floor
Pittsburgh, PA 15224

As a pediatric nurse, healthcare executive and an individual who has experienced a personal and tragic loss in my life, I have found Maggie's story nothing less than extremely hopeful, powerful, and transformational. Her story restores a parent's faith that there is life after the loss of a child.

Maggie's remarkable story of "tangible hearts" coming to her in so many ways allows us to consider that our deceased children, like angels, are always with us despite the grief, anger and sorrow one may be experiencing after such a tragic loss.

As a health care provider, I thank Maggie for her time, commitment and support in sharing her story over and over again with our grieving parents at the Children's Hospital of Pittsburgh of the University of Pittsburgh Medical Center. I realize this may be just one small step in their journey toward recovery, but it is a step toward loving and living again.

Maggie…you are an inspiration!

Diane S. Hupp, MSN, RN, NEA-BC
Vice President, Patient Care Services & Chief Nursing Officer
Children's Hospital of Pittsburgh of UPMC
4401 Penn Avenue
Pittsburgh, PA 15224

I met Maggie Horgan seven months after my eleven-year-old daughter, Maggie, died from Ewing's sarcoma (the same cancer that took Neil's life). Only God could have orchestrated our meeting. I believe our children, heavenly friends, found a way for their moms to meet so we could support each other. I was given a heart-shaped rock from a family friend with Maggie's business card attached to it. The heart rock gift started an important friendship between two moms who understand living with the sorrow of the loss of a child.

The unexplainable ways our children continue to connect with us give us hope, comfort, and a glimpse of heaven. The resounding message, "I am with you still," echoes through my being with each connection. Thank you for writing about your journey with heart rocks, Maggie. Your story is a beautiful confirmation of the enduring love between mother and child. The amazing ways that God reveals Himself through these connections with our children gives us the grace to carry on.

Sincerely,

Cyndi McGinnis
Ligonier, PA

Having attended the CHP Memorial Services over the years, I am always struck at the strength of our guest speakers and what they bring to our grieving families. Maggie's story is inspiring and heart-wrenching, but the message is clear: through the ups and downs, the self-doubt and pain, you just don't know when something is going to touch you both physically and spiritually. As Maggie speaks and the heart stone is passed around, there is a physical buzz that can be felt by our families. They can see that there is some light in the distance—that there is hope. Although not all bereaved families will receive hearts, Maggie's story tells us that they will receive whatever they need. They will survive their immense loss.

Michael Shulock, MS, CCLS
Certified Child Life Specialist II
Hematology/Oncology Clinic-9C
Child Life Internship Co-Coordinator
Children's Hospital of Pittsburgh of UPMC
4401 Penn Ave, Pittsburgh, PA 15224

My husband and I first met Maggie Horgan about seven months after our beloved eight-year-old daughter, Shannon, left this earth. Her death was caused by a freak accident at home. As her mother, I didn't believe I would survive the horror of her leaving us.

At the time, Maggie was a featured speaker during a memorial service we attended at the Children's Hospital of Pittsburgh. Shannon was one of the children being remembered that day. I could not help but pay attention.

Like Maggie, and her heart stone connection to Neil, I had been experiencing a similar connection to my own deceased child. In my case, I often felt an uncanny awareness that my Shannon was near, and each time it happened was marked by my also finding a dime! This seemed strange to me, even though I had heard and read of such phenomena being significant following the loss of a loved one. I knew finding dimes from my deceased child seemed like a crazy idea, but just in case my little girl was reaching out to me, I clung to the concept. For me, each and every one of those silly dimes was salve on the raw wounds I felt grief had inflicted upon me.

Maggie's heart stone story resonated with me right away, especially since it validated my dimes, but my husband remained a little skeptical. This seemed funny to me because we had already found two dimes that very morning...before Maggie ever uttered a word. My husband was entitled to his perspective, but when I found a *third* dime at his feet (which had not been there when we took our seats) I knew Maggie's words included a message I had yet to fully understand. In short, I felt connected to this woman who I had never met before.

After the service ended, I introduced myself to Maggie and gave her one of the three dimes my husband and I had discovered that morning. I also thanked her for courageously sharing her pain, but more so for her willingness to share hope. *I needed hope.* Like all the days since Shannon's accident, I had arrived at the special service with a heavy heart. Despite the foundation of faith I had been raised with, my daughter's death left it somewhat shattered. I was at the end of my rope in many ways when I arrived at Children's that day, but Maggie's speech tied a knot at the end of it for me. Little did she know, she gave me something to hang on to.

About ten months later, I found a heart-shaped stone of my own, and I knew Shannon's spirit had sent it. Perhaps Neil's did, too. I held on to that stone tightly, and it became an important part of my healing toolbox (and like many other grieving parents, I needed all the tools I could get). In my quest to continue with this effort, I signed up for many spiritual classes, one of them at the Nuin Centre in Pittsburgh's East End. As the class progressed, I felt certain I knew the beautiful woman who was seated behind me, yet I could not remember where we had met or why.

During a break, I approached the woman and asked her how we might know each other. She seemed stumped, and I could tell by her reply that she wasn't sure we knew each other at all. But hearing her voice was all I needed. It triggered my memory immediately.

I suddenly knew exactly who the vaguely familiar woman was and said to her, "You are the heart stone mom!"

Maggie chucked and replied, "You *do* know me."

I responded, "I'm the dime mom!"

Then we hugged. *Of course we hugged!* And as we did, I'm confident that Neil and Shannon both smiled.

I am happy to offer this testimonial for Maggie, and I am also proud of her for completing this journey to lightness. Her words gave me hope when I had little. Her faith opened the door of possibilities for my own healing wider than I could open it by myself.

Sincerely,

Sherri L. Wilson
Pittsburgh, PA

I have been working in palliative care and end of life care for 15 years. For the last 10 years, I have been specifically caring for pediatric patients and their families. In my current role as Manager of the Supportive Care Program at Children's Hospital of Pittsburgh of UPMC I have had the opportunity to hear Maggie Horgan's incredible story about heart stones. Maggie has shared her story at our Bi-Annual memorial service on many occasions. And I have to admit; every time she speaks I gain more insight concerning grief.

For me, there is no more important care I can provide (as a nurse) than to care for a person at the end of his or her life. I find it both an honor and a blessing to walk this journey with my patients and their families. I believe I have learned something valuable from each of my patient and family interactions; consequently, the insight I have gained along the way has allowed me to provide a more comprehensive type of care to all my patients. For instance, when families of children who are dying ask me how other families "get through," one way I answer that question is to share Maggie's story. I tell them about her heartifacts.

Maggie's walk into the Pacific Ocean, which occurred one month after her son died, became the avenue through which she could finally express her grief. Her sharing of that walk has helped others, but it also allowed the people she knew—or would come to know—a way to offer their support to her in return. Grief is a complex journey that must be traveled, despite our best attempts to skip past it. By sharing Maggie's story, I feel I am able to give parents who face the loss of their child a sliver of confidence, hope. Her story reveals a light at the end of the very long tunnel grieving parents are forced to face.

Carol May, RN, MSN, MBA, CHPN
Manager, Supportive Care
Children's Hospital of Pittsburgh of UPMC
4401 Penn Avenue
Pittsburgh, PA, 15224